WITHDRAWN

Pals, Pranks and Perils
Learning Life's Lessons in the 1930s

Eldon Ralph Weaver

Dedication

In memory of my parents, Benjamin Opdyke Weaver and Harriet Marietta Marriage Weaver, who provided my sisters, brother, and me a perfect childhood, despite the troubles and worries during the ten years of the Great Depression and the Dust Bowl era.

In memory of my adoring older sister, Vivian, who become a prolific writer of her memoirs during her eighties and inspired me to continue writing my stories.

Table Of Contents

Contents

Acknowledgments

My daughter, Trudy, urged me to continue writing about my favorite memories from my childhood. She assisted with editing and preserved family photos for the illustrations and cover design. Her time and help has been invaluable in completing this book.

Cover Design:
Canyon landscape at Eagle Canyon Ranch
Eldon riding Toots, his favorite horse c. 1939

Preface

My first experience in writing a short story about my childhood was in the 1980s when I wrote about my cousin who was shirking on his share of the ranch work and how we threw him into the hog wallow for punishment. It was a funny story to look back on and I found that others enjoyed reading it. That experience encouraged me to write about other humorous, exciting, or unique experiences from my childhood. I grew up on a large ranch near Mullinville, Kansas during the 1930s and there were plenty of events and unusual people who came and went from the ranch over the years.

My grandfather, John Marriage, wrote his memoirs in the early 1900s. Then, my mother began writing her memories and short stories as she aspired to become an author. She found time to write and publish articles and short stories while raising a family of five children, handling the ranch bookkeeping, pursuing her interests in family history and genealogy, and supporting my father in his career as a rancher and state representative.

There is something comforting in knowing about one's family history and having a sense of place and significance. The gift of a legacy of writing is hard to describe. I felt the urge to continue our family tradition of writing our memoirs. I was further inspired by my sister, Vivian, who wrote many stories about our family and her entire life experience through the Depression, Dirty Thirties and World War II.

As I wrote and shared more of my stories, I realized how much I enjoyed writing and how much my family and friends enjoyed reading my tales. Some of the stories I told my children when they were small had been forgotten, so they encouraged me to add those episodes to my collection. The flood of happy memories brought all of us great pleasure and laughs.

Reflecting on one's past can be either happy or sad, depending on how one chooses to hold those memories. Of course, there were sad times, failures, and unfulfilled dreams. I learned from my parents to take life as it comes and make the best of the situation. We can't control our circumstances but we can control how we respond to them. Along with a deep, abiding faith in the love of God, that philosophy has served me well in my adult life and I hope I have passed that on to my children and grandchildren.

CHAPTER ONE

A Colorful Character Arrives at Eagle Canyon Ranch

Life on a farm or ranch has always been one of long hours, hard work, unpredictable weather, and hazardous jobs. But ranching during the 1930s was far beyond the natural cycle of seasons. The Great Depression and the Dust Bowl days set records that still stand in history and still stand out in old-time farmers' memories. As a young boy in those days, I didn't realize how hard it was on everyone. No one had any money and it seemed that we were all in the same tough situation.

I grew up on big cattle ranch established in 1898 by my grandfather, John Marriage, in Kiowa County, Kansas. He left Iowa with his wife and two children and a small herd of prize cattle to start a ranch in western Kansas. My mother, Marietta, was nine years old and her brother, Ira, was seven years old at the time. The family traveled by covered wagon and lived in a lean-to tent for almost two years after arriving in Kansas. They struggled against droughts, blizzards, coyotes, rattlesnakes, and financial troubles. Gradually, they bought land and developed a ranch of ten thousand acres. John built up a large herd of his own purebred cattle, Marriage Mulleys, that became famous across the state of Kansas. He built a twenty-four room ranch house and due to his foresight, it had running water, three full bathrooms, and flush toilets. It was built into the south side of a deep canyon located nine miles south of Mullinville, Kansas. Grandfather had the water well drilled on a canyon bank, twenty-two feet

higher than the house. The well was two hundred and ten feet deep and in a vein of water thirty feet in depth, providing a bountiful supply of cold, pure water. An Aeromotor Windmill provided the pumping power and a two hundred gallon enclosed tank served as a reservoir of fresh water when there was no wind. Gravity pressure was plenty adequate to provide water pressure for use in the bathrooms, kitchen, and for laundry.

Grandfather Marriage died after a Model T accident in 1923, so my father took over management of the ranch and cattle breeding on behalf of the Marriage Mulley Cattle Company, of which my parents, Mama's brother, and my grandmother were partners. Uncle Ira, or Ira J, as Mama called him, wasn't interested in the family business, but rather had a passion for machines, equipment, and developing his own inventions. By the time I was born in 1927, the ranch was five thousand acres. Papa was raising and selling Marriage Mulley bulls and cows, selling cream, and raising wheat, hogs, and sorghum for silage.

I was the youngest child of five. My oldest sister, Marjorie, was thirteen years older than me and she went off to college before I can remember. I was only three years old at the time. Vivian was eleven years older than me and was a senior in high school when I was in first grade. We called Vivian "Diddy" because my next sister, Doris, couldn't say "Vivian" when she was small. Doris was eight years older. For a few years, Doris had the nickname "Boardy" because I couldn't pronounce Doris. My brother, Kenny, was almost six years older. He was enough older than me that he thought I was just a nuisance and pest who bothered him when he wanted to do grown-up things with his friends. Once in a while he pulled me around the yard in my red wagon. And even though Uncle Ira and his family lived nearby on the ranch, my cousins, L.J., Lois, and Marilyn, were much older, too.

During the summer of 1932, Mr. Vanetti, a good neighbor of ours, telephoned my father, Ben Weaver, at Eagle Canyon Ranch and told him that a World War One veteran had wandered onto his farm. Mr. Vanetti said the man was homeless, nearly broke, and looking for work. He was willing to work for his room and board just to have a roof over his head and something to eat.

Mr. Vanetti knew there was always plenty of work at Eagle Canyon Ranch. The five thousand acre ranch always had fields to plow or plant, fence and corral repairs, and cattle chores of feeding, putting to pasture, or checking the windmills and stock tanks for water. Vanetti said the man was a steady farm hand, willing to do most any job from daylight until dark. Most of all he enjoyed driving the tractor. His name was Willet T. Allen. The "T" stood for Theodore as he was named after former President Theodore Roosevelt. Mr. Vanetti no longer needed a hired hand that summer since all of Mr. Vanetti's land had been worked and he had no cattle to tend or fences to repair.

Mr. Vanetti offered to bring Bill, as he preferred to be called, to the ranch and Papa agreed to give Bill a job by the month. The pay would be thirty dollars a month plus room and board. Bill was over forty years old at the time but he looked even older. He stood about five feet eight inches tall and was husky and barrel-chested. He had a slightly protruding belly even though he did manual labor all day. His unkempt hair was a reddish-blond and was beginning to thin on top. Bill usually had a few days growth of reddish whiskers because he hated to shave and only did so once a week.

My first introduction to Bill upon his arrival was as Kenny was pushing me lickety-split around the yard in the old red wagon. As we whizzed around the corner of the ranch house, we nearly collided with Bill and Papa as they walked across the yard from the truck to the front room door. Bill seemed shocked to see us. He frowned down at us and in a gruff, disapproving voice said, "I didn't know there was any kids in the family." Papa introduced us to Bill by our names and ages; Kenny, age ten, and little Eldon, age five.

In the early Thirties, the economic and financial woes of the Depression were intense. The stock market crash of 1929 caused businesses to close and men lost their jobs. Farmers tried to grow more crops to pay their bills but prices dropped as more wheat, cattle, and hogs flooded the market. Money was scarce and most of our hired ranch hands and field workers with families had moved on in search of better paying work. The lack of cash meant that Papa couldn't pay wages so Bill was provided room, board, and clothing in return for his labor. A cash monthly payment was to follow when the hard times ended and the cash-strapped farmers and ranchers could pay wages. Bill was assigned to live in the basement level of the ranch house where there were vacant apartments for hired hands and he was to eat all meals with our family upstairs.

One of the daily chores assigned to Bill was milking five or six of the big, red, hornless Marriage Mulley cows every morning and evening. He seemed to like the routine of going to the barn twice a day to milk the cows, then hauling the fresh milk down the hill to the ranch house, and running the milk through the hand-cranked De Laval milk separator. Whole milk was strained and put in the huge ice box along with the cream for household use. Carrying two full milk pails nearly a quarter mile from the milk barn to the house was a

chore in itself. Then, Bill dutifully hauled the buckets of skimmed milk back up the hill to the barn to feed the chickens and pigs.

Once all the daily chores were completed, Bill cranked up the "Johnny-Pop" John Deere tractor, so named because of the popping sound of the two cylinder tractor engine, and idled off to do field work. By then, the Model D John Deere lug tractor had replaced the use of mules in harness for plowing. My grandfather loved to use mules on the ranch in the early 1900s and into the 1920s because of their sure-footed ability to traverse the canyons. Bill could be seen bouncing up and down on the steel spring seat, puffing on a pipe filled with Prince Albert tobacco. He loved to spend the day driving the tractor, bouncing along pulling a one-way disc or a three-bottom moldboard plow from early morning till dusk.

Bill soon fell into a routine of rising early to milk the cows and then doing field work, mending fence, or seeing to other repairs around the barns and windmills. He joined us for dinner each evening after washing up from his chores and donning a clean pair of bib overalls. Bill had a huge appetite, continuing to eat as long as any food was left on the platters or in the bowls covering our large dining room table. If any child complained about some food item, Bill would exclaim, "You'll be mighty lucky if'n you don't see a lot worse a-foren you're my age."

Mama and Grandma Marriage didn't approve of his tobacco habit and especially hated his tobacco-stained bib overalls. The faded denim bib was streaked with dark, reddish brown tobacco stains from his chest to his waist, and sometimes onto his pant legs. The dirt and grease from his ranch chores seemed to permanently set the tobacco stains. And his habit of shaving once a week added to his bedraggled appearance.

Gradually, we all became better acquainted with Bill as we attempted to overlook his gruff, cantankerous personality and his personal habits. Kenny and I were taken aback by his crotchety demeanor and tried to steer clear of him at first. Vivian, a junior in high school, and Doris, a freshman, seemed to know just how to overcome his pessimistic attitude. The girls were fun-loving and kidded with Bill frequently, noting how much he relished attention. They seemed to have a secret game to see which one could get him to smile most often. Bill was a good sport and occasionally smiled when something was especially humorous or delighted him. He never had much to say in our conversations and kept his emotions to himself. Even when especially happy or disgusted, he only had a few words or could be heard grumbling to himself about the problem. My oldest sister, Marjorie, met Bill when she came home for the summer from attending Kansas State Teacher's College in Emporia. She soon became part of the girls' joking and teasing with Bill.

Gradually, I could see that Bill had a good heart under his tough exterior. Having been introduced to him as Bill Allen, my sisters soon nicknamed him "Blallen" much to his delight. It was the fastest way to say Bill Allen in one word.

Mama learned from Bill that his mother died when he and his brother, Art, were just boys. Their stepmother resented the boys and made their lives miserable while they were growing up in Nebraska. When Bill was older and a big, strapping youth, he ran away from home and lied about his age to find work. When the draft came along, he enlisted and joined the Army. He served in France during

World War One in 1917 and 1918. Mama was sympathetic to Bill's skepticism and pessimistic outlook after realizing he had suffered a lot of hurt in his younger years. He was accustomed to being a loner but made the best of his situation. His pessimism was evident when Papa or Mama greeted him with a "Good morning, Bill. Isn't it a pretty day?" His usual gruff response was, "It won't be this nice tomorrow."

A kind gesture can reach a wound that only compassion can heal.

CHAPTER TWO

A Fiery Ordeal

During the summer months, my older sister, Marjorie, was home from college and Vivian and Doris spent harvest days at home on the ranch while school wasn't in session. They were a great help to Mama with all the household chores of cooking, washing dishes, and cleaning the house. And there were a multitude of duties required to feed hungry harvest crews of as many as twenty-four men plus the numerous city cousins and visitors. It was always fun to have my sisters at home to give me a lot of special attention.

Mama was away from the ranch to attend her Bon Trés Club meeting in Mullinville, leaving Marj in charge of us and responsible for cooking supper. Ranch meals were always prepared on a Coleman gasoline cook stove which was a cleaner, faster heat than kerosene. Gasoline ranges required heating the generator which then vaporized the gasoline before lighting the main burners.

The procedure to start the stove was to use three tablespoons of kerosene from a covered tin can stored in the pantry. Marj spooned the kerosene into the reservoir, lighted it with a wooden match, and waited for the usual blue burner flame to be lighted. Nothing happened to light the stove, so Marj grabbed the kerosene can again and dipped out another tablespoon and spooned it into the reservoir.

Marj didn't notice that there were still some flames in the reservoir and as she returned the flaming spoon to the kerosene can, a fiery flame leaped up. She hastily grabbed the burning kerosene can and started for the kitchen door, hoping to get the flaming can outdoors. But the flames heated the metal can and it instantly was too hot to handle. Marj dropped the can and the flaming fuel spread over the entire kitchen floor. She shrieked, "Fire! Fire!" in hopes of attracting someone to come to the rescue.

Her shouts quickly got my attention. I ran to the kitchen and seeing the kitchen engulfed in flames, the fear and escape emotions of a five-year-old were triggered. I dashed out the front door and ran full speed up the long hill all the way to the windmill before stopping. Fortunately, Vivian and Doris rushed to the kitchen to help Marj fight the perilous fire.

The fear of fire at the ranch house had always been a part of our family's foresight and precautions. Great-grandfather Marriage had a large bell of cast iron from the C. S. Bell Company installed at the

 house. It was to be rung whenever there was an emergency. The clear, piercing ring from the crystal metal bell carried for miles across the prairies. When it rang, all the ranch hands and cowboys were instructed to come to the house to help. He worried about having water to fight a fire if one broke out when there had been no wind to fill the huge water tank that supplied the house. But, Great-grandfather's back up plan was to keep cream cans filled with water that were used in the kitchen for cooking purposes. As luck would have it, we had been two days without the gusty, strong Kansas wind to activate the windmill which resulted in no water pumped and no water in the tank.

Vivian and Doris rushed to the kitchen and instinctively each one grabbed a cream can and dashed the flames with gallons of water. What a relief when the last flame flickered out. Cleaning up the smelly kerosene mess by mopping the water and tending to the slight burns to Marjorie's right hand were the only repercussions of a near disaster.

A second close call with fire had occurred just a few weeks earlier. Cousin Elmer Rusco, who we nicknamed Peter Rabbit, and I were pretending that we were camping in the double garage located about one hundred feet from the ranch house. We had watched Papa fill a portable, square camp stove with fuel, light a match, and then a bright blue flame flickered above the wide wick. I suggested to Peter Rabbit, "Let's fill the camp stove from the gasoline barrel."

"Sounds like fun, Eldon," he agreed. The gasoline barrel in the garage held two hundred gallons and was used to fuel the cars and truck. Little did we know, at ages five or six, that gasoline was highly flammable. The barrel had a spigot in the end and laid horizontally on a heavy wood stand. As we opened the spigot, out came a gushing stream of gasoline that overflowed the smaller opening on the neck on the stove. In no time, there was excess gasoline running in all directions on the concrete garage floor.

We put the stove down and ran to the house as I explained to Peter Rabbit, "We have to get the wood matches that are in the

kitchen." Mama kept the wood matches in a tin matchbox mounted high on the kitchen cabinet wall. She had warned all of us over and over, "Never play with matches," but those warnings seemed to have disappeared from our minds as we climbed the stepstool and grabbed a handful of matches. We dashed back to the garage to light the stove. As soon as we struck the first match, a flame shot upward and scorched our hair and hands.

Fire immediately spread over the garage floor coming just inches from the big gasoline barrel. We were panic-stricken and in pain from the burns on our hands. We ran to the house and I was screaming, "Mama, Mama, quick! Fire! Fire!" I was terrified as I pointed toward the garage. She dashed out the screen door and ran to the fire bell mounted in the fork of the lone cottonwood tree in the front yard. She pulled the rope a half-dozen times and the crystal metal bell sounded its clear, loud alarm across the landscape. Blallen and another hired hand heard it and came running down the hill from the barn. They dashed into the garage, grabbed old tarps, and threw them over the flames which smothered the fire before the flames reached the gasoline barrel.

I was so traumatized that I didn't need the scolding we received from Mama and Aunt Bertie about playing with matches. And we got some more words from Blallen. "You crazy kids," he growled. "That barrel of gasoline has more blasting power than two sticks of dynamite!" Peter Rabbit and I were two remorseful and thankful little boys after Blallen scolded us. The real danger finally sank in.

For weeks I was afraid to go to sleep at night as I imagined the house catching on fire. As a pre-schooler, I sometimes had scary dreams which awoke me in the night. Diddy would let me sleep with her until I was all settled in again and sound asleep. One such night, instead of waking me to go back downstairs to my bedroom, Diddy tried to carry me down the long flight of stairs. She had on soft, thin anklets and lost her footing on the slippery, varnished stair treads. We bounced down the last three steps and she injured herself in her efforts to keep from dropping me.

I always felt badly about that incident when she injured herself while putting my welfare above hers. I did learn a lifetime lesson about not getting into something I was told to stay away from and not playing with matches.

A wise man is guided by prudent rules.

CHAPTER THREE

The Dipping of Peter Rabbit

Elmer and Bill Rusco, my first cousins, came to live at Eagle Canyon Ranch when they were six and ten years old and I was seven years old. Their mother, Aunt Bertie, was Papa's widowed older sister who needed a place to live and help to feed her two growing boys. Times were especially hard as the Depression dragged on and unemployment was affecting so many families. My folks always helped anyone in need and invited the Ruscos to live in an apartment on the second floor of the four-story ranch house.

Elmer had a favorite pair of floppy Peter Rabbit house slippers that he always wore just before bedtime. Papa was like an adopted father to the boys and the highlight of their day was to take a "horsey-back" ride by sitting on Papa's broad, strong shoulders with their legs straddling his neck. Papa would flop Elmer's feet up and down while prancing through the ranch house. Soon the Peter Rabbit slippers would fly off his feet, into the air, and across the room, much to Elmer's delight. He soon acquired the nickname of Peter Rabbit Rusco, later shortened to Pete. Papa gave Bill the nickname, Woolo, due to his curly, short brown hair.

Later that spring, Pete developed an irritating rash that was breaking out all over his back and legs. He was constantly scratching and digging at his red, rough welts and causing even more irritation. Papa had treated farm animals over the years for a variety of ailments, including lice and mange, with his favorite medication. It was a concoction of creosote dip. Since none of Aunt Bertie's remedies had helped Pete, Papa decided that a good dipping was the only answer to Pete's demise. He explained to Pete, "Dip is a mighty fine remedy and cures nearly all types of skin ailments. Now, wouldn't you like to be cured of all that itching and scratching?"

Pete solemnly but hesitantly nodded his agreement so we headed for the milk cow barn where the Kreso Dip was stored. Papa mixed up a gallon of the strong-smelling, milky solution and had Pete strip off his overalls and shorts there in the cow barn. Papa slowly began pouring the potent dip down Pete's  back, beginning at his neckline, and rubbing the mixture into the welts and rash that covered his back and legs. On Pete's ankles were some particularly red and raw spots which he had scratched until there were open sores in patches the size of a dime. When that powerful dip seeped into those spots, Pete felt it burning and thought he was on fire.

He let out a shriek, bolting out of the cow barn stark naked and hollering at the top of his lungs. All we could see was Pete running lickety-split across the barnyard. He was the first and last birthday-suit runner we ever saw on Eagle Canyon Ranch. Somehow he had enough sense to leap into the big horse watering tank between the barn and the house. The cool water soon stopped the burning sensation and Pete calmed down considerably.

It was amazing to us that within a few hours Pete's itching had subsided and a week later his welts had nearly disappeared. Later on, Pete quoted his Uncle Benny by proudly saying, "Heavenly days. My skin is as slick and smooth as a mole's hide!" We decided that every medicine chest should have an ample supply of creosote dip, cow salve, and maybe some wormer.

While helping Aunt Bertie clean up her apartment, my mother discovered the culprits and cause for Pete's terrible rash. He had those awful bed bugs. They had infested the old cotton mattress Aunt Bertie brought along to the ranch for Pete. It was immediately cremated in a trash pile away from the house, followed by a treatment of kerosene for the bed frame and springs. With a new mattress and gradually diminishing kerosene fumes, Pete soon had bite-free, peaceful dreams.

Sometimes the remedy is worse than the ailment.

CHAPTER FOUR

L. J. and the Model A Ford

We rarely saw automobiles on the rough, rutted dirt roads in the country, especially in the vicinity of Eagle Canyon Ranch, located in the buffalo grass canyon-land nine miles from the nearest town. Consequently, it was exciting for us as seven- and eight-year-olds when any motorized vehicle appeared on the horizon approaching the ranch house.

Even more exciting was when our twenty-year-old cousin, L. J. Marriage, came whizzing down the hill in his shiny black 1929 Model A Ford coupe with a fold-open rumble seat. Following a hasty greeting, L. J. would shout above the clattering engine noise, "Who wants to take a ride in the rumble seat?" He could barely finish the invitation before Peter Rabbit, Woolo, and I climbed into the rumble seat for a thrilling ride. Aunt Bertie was terrorized by L. J.'s wild driving and would come rushing out of the ranch house shouting over and over, "Someone save my children!" L. J.'s heavy foot on the gas pedal increased the engine roar, quickly drowning out her plea. In those days, we knew nothing about the impact of speed and had no safety precautions for passengers in motorized vehicles.

L. J. and the Model A Ford

We didn't know that L. J. had quite a reputation for his wild driving. Before Mullinville had school buses, he drove the Essex to town school in 1927 with Marjorie, Vivian, Doris and his sister, Lois, on board. They often complained of his wild driving. He seemed to love terrifying the girls as he roared down the hill to the house and hit the brakes. He threw the car into a fast swerve to avoid hitting the  hitching post. The rear end of the big Essex slid sideways and tossed the girls into each others' laps while barely avoiding a crash into the garage. Another time he ran off the road while going too fast in a curve. The big Essex ran over a culvert and overturned but no one was seriously hurt. The girls eventually decided not to ride with him and his fun with them was over.

Once we three boys were loaded into the Model A, L. J. would drive down into the deep canyon valley behind the ranch house watching for a fairly smooth canyon bank without too many humps. Once located, he would tromp down on the gas pedal and as he said, "I'll put the pedal to the metal," and gain all the speed possible before shooting straight up the canyon wall. He held on the gas until the Model A climbed as high as possible on the canyon wall before the wheels spun out and lost traction. Then, he would put in the clutch, allowing us to speed backward lickety-split down the canyon wall to the canyon valley floor. Wow—what a thrill! Something we never before experienced when riding a horse or mule. It was better than any circus ride we knew about and much better than swinging or riding a merry-go-round. After one such event, I confided in Peter Rabbit that someday I was going to own a Model A Ford with a rumble seat.

Do all you can to make your dreams come true.

CHAPTER FIVE

My Hometown of Mullinville, Kansas

One of the many exciting experiences while growing up on Eagle Canyon Ranch in the early 1930s was an occasional automobile trip to the nearest town, our hometown of Mullinville, Kansas. It was nine miles on a rough and dusty country road and quite a bouncy ride in the old '29 Chevy sedan. Consequently, a number of errands were completed on each trip.

Located in western Kansas on 154 Highway, Mullinville was a farming community with about four hundred residents during the 1930s. Another five thousand people lived in other towns and the surrounding area of Kiowa County. Papa would take me with him as we visited a variety of establishments up and down the three block business district on Main Street. These visits, in the eyes of an eight-year-old, were not only exciting but memorable. Each proprietor had a different personality that left a lasting impression upon me.

Our first stop as we came into town from the south was the Rock Island Depot where we typically delivered a five-gallon can of cream to be shipped to the Galva Creamery in Kansas City. We always milked five or six of our family-originated cattle breed, the Marriage Mulleys. Their milk supplied our family and the ranch hands with fresh milk, separator cream, and butter. The skimmed milk was fed to

Mullinville Depot

the hogs and chickens and the surplus cream was sold for a little extra but much needed cash and shipped by rail from Mullinville

Mr. Carl Oney, the Rock Island Depot Agent, was a friendly Missourian with an unusual twang to his speech and many colloquial expressions. It intrigued me to listen to him talk. He kept my attention when he donned his green celluloid visor cap, sat down at the wooden desk that faced the railroad tracks, and tapped out a message with his telegraph key using Railroad Telegrapher's Code. The Oneys had two sons, Doug and Jerry, and lived in a part of the depot. Amazingly, they slept soundly when the fast flyer and freight trains whizzed by the depot throughout the night. The rail depot was an important part of the community. In those days, trains hauled ninety per cent of the freight and goods across the country long before there were semi-trailer trucks. Carl often had to stand up on the telegraph pole during wheat harvest to watch for the signal light out of Bucklin, eight miles away, to turn red. Then he could get the tracks cleared of wheat trucks in time for the train to pass by on the main track. Before the crossing gates were common, Carl typically had to flag the Main Street crossing as there were a few collisions.

The Jesus Espinosa family lived just east of the Rock Island Depot in two freight cars. One car was used for a living area and the other used for bedroom space. Their box cars were on the rail siding but next to the main railroad track which made for a noisy home when the flyer and freights whizzed by day and night. Mr. Espinosa was a hard worker as a railroad section hand, trying to support his large family on a lowly wage. Working three hundred and sixty-five days a year in rain, sleet, or snow, he helped lay new crossties and maintained the railroad track. There was very little money left after buying food for the family of six children. My friend, Eulalio, was my age and the fourth of their six children.

Shoes were a relatively expensive item even during the Depression, and the Espinosas usually were in need of new shoes that were the right sizes. Papa well remembered sharing shoes with his older sister as a child so he and Bertha could take turns going to school, and he was very sympathetic of the Espinosa's plight. Periodically, Papa would stop by the Espinosa's and inquire which children needed shoes the most at that particular time. He carried a light piece of cardboard along and would trace around the feet of the child or children most in need, then use the drawing for sizing at the shoe store. Papa loved to see their dark eyes light up and their bright smiles when he returned with new shoes for them.

The Equity Exchange Co-Op office, located across Main Street from the depot and right next to the Rock Island railroad tracks, handled records of thousands of bushels of wheat stored in the huge concrete elevators. Papa liked to stop in to visit with Mr. Ernest French, the manager, and check on the current price of wheat, in hopes it would rise above a dollar and twenty-five cents a bushel so he could sell at a profit. Mr. French was an efficient manager and the first person I had ever heard who was a stutterer. He was friendly and visited with Papa, talking along normally. Then suddenly, Mr. French would get stalled on the first

letter of a word and repeat it several times before blurting out the full word and then continuing on with the conversation. I was spellbound and almost wanted to say the word for him. While I didn't know much about stuttering as a child, it made me realize that anyone can be different. My dad didn't seem to be bothered by it nor should I.

Bill Sluder's blacksmith shop was the next stop. His large cement-block shop was filled overhead with a maze of shafts, various pulleys, and belts driving a variety of blacksmithing power hammers, grinders, and drills. It was dimly lit by exterior windows and had a unique smell of machinery and a coal burning forge. There were always plow shares and one-way discs needing to be sharpened in addition to implement parts needing to be welded. Bill was a tall, stout man clad in blue overalls. No shirt was needed due to the intense and blazing heat of the forge that he kept fired up all day. His upper arm muscles fairly rippled with each blow of his heavy blacksmith hammer on the one hundred pound solid steel anvil. He pounded out the edges of a cherry red plow share pulled with tongs directly from the hot forge. Mrs. Sluder, Florence, was a small, comely lady. She was equipped with a paper tablet and pencil and wrote down each customer's needs and requests for repairs. She also kept their books and attempted to collect from each customer as they stopped by to pick up their supplies or repaired equipment. During the Depression, it was sometimes hard to collect a bill from a farmer who had hardscrabble land with no crop to sell. Bill had two huge, cylindrical tanks on a heavy steel-wheeled cart for his carbide and acetylene to power his welder. Before lighting his torch, he always cautioned kids to look the other way when he welded to protect their eyes from a piece of flying

MAP OF MULLINVILLE
AND LOCAL BUSINESSES
c. 1935

A Coffee Shop
B Drug Store
C First State Bank
D Barber Shop
E Jock Nolan's Garage
F Sinclair & Hardware
G High School
H Post Office
I Mullinville News

J Sager's Grocery
K Equity Exchange
L Elevators
M Depot
N Sluder's Blacksmith
O Telegraph Office
P Sayer's Grocery
Q Lunchroom (school)

metal or to avoid the injury from the intense, bright blue flame. I soon learned how important a blacksmith was in keeping farm equipment repaired and in operating order.

A stop at Wright's Drug Store on 154 Highway, just west of the First State Bank, was a real treat for me. Mr. Wright, a small bald-headed man, was the soda jerk while his wife operated the pharmacy. In those days, the soda jerk prepared special concoctions of milk, ice cream, carbonated water and flavored syrups for

Drug Store

customers. Charlie was noted for watery milk shakes and malts in his efforts to save on the more costly ice cream. Papa always ordered strawberry malts for each of us and encouraged Charlie to put in plenty of ice cream, noting that we already had more than enough milk at the ranch. Those cold, sweet, and fruity malts were a delightful treat on a hot, windy Kansas day during the Dust Bowl years.

Dwight Harp's Hardware and Sinclair Service Station was across the highway from Wright's Drugstore. We never bought gasoline there since it was cheaper at the Co-Op Service Station. Dwight was a rather gruff-voiced proprietor who wore baggy unkempt clothing. He usually had the bolts, nuts, nails, or fence staples we need for repairs at the ranch. Ironically, Miss Bertha Peebler, a neat and precise Home

Charlie Sherer & Dwight Harp

Economics teacher, later married Dwight. George Webber, an easy-going clerk at the hardware store, was comical and usually had some funny words of wisdom. I thought it was hilarious when he always referred to a car's glove compartment as a bloomer box.

Bill Allen, our trusty farm hand, enjoyed loafing at Harp's Sinclair Service Station on Sunday. Bill smoked a pipe and fit right in with the fellows at the service station. Bill enjoyed the conversation while the Weaver family attended Sunday school and church at the United Brethren Church. He would take Sunday as a day of rest, take his weekly bath, shave, put on clean overalls and shirt, and ride to Mullinville with the family. While the family was at church, Blallen would loaf and visit at the service station until church let out, then ride home again. Much to my folks' regret, in all the years he worked at the ranch, they were unable to get Blallen to set foot in the church.

United Brethren Church

Next door and north of Wright's Drug Store was Lloyd Casper's Barber Shop where Papa would occasionally stop for a haircut.

Keggie, as some customers called Lloyd, probably due to his plump, barrel-chested body shape resembling a beer keg, kept his customers updated on all the latest local happenings. Keggie later added pool tables for customers to play a game for twenty-five cents while they waited for their turn in the barber chair. Later on, Keggie bought two combines, hiring operators to follow the wheat harvest. Ben Brown, a small, bald-headed witty farmer, enjoyed heckling Keggie with such remarks as, "Keggie, if you made one round around a patch of wheat, would you charge a poor farmer for cutting the whole field?"

"Of course not," Keggie would reply.

Ben then retorted, "Then why do you charge me full price for cutting a little fringe of hair around my bald head?" Keggie reportedly never took such remarks favorably.

His apprentice barber was a tall, lanky, wavy-haired guy named Glen Tanner, who quietly snipped away the customer's hair and listened to the ramblings in the next chair. Later, Glen married Miss Elsie Crouch, called Miss Grouch by us kids behind her back, who truly was a remarkable music teacher. She tried to instill a desire for singing in our grade school music class. She played the piano well and let us choose songs to sing from our dark-green music book entitled, *America's Favorites*. Some of our favorites included *My Old Kentucky Home, Bless This House, My Grandfather's Clock, Old Black Joe,* and *Long, Long Ago*. She would craftily insert a new song for us to learn in between our favorites. I attributed our class members' life-long enjoyment of music and knowledge of notes to her dedicated efforts.

Alfred "Jock" Nolan operated a car repair shop across Main Street east of the barbershop. As he worked on vehicles, he smoked a black pipe that was covered with grease from his hands. Jock spent considerable time tamping his pipe with Prince Albert tobacco before puffing away. He spent full-time keeping local cars and trucks repaired and in service. Papa would take the old Chevy in to Jock when it developed some sort of ailment. Jock was a prankster; one of his favorite tricks was to charge a car condenser, then lay it on the greasy counter where customers came to pay their bills. Curiosity usually overcame a waiting customer who couldn't resist picking up the condenser for closer scrutiny. The minute a finger touched the protruding wire, a powerful jolt of electricity discharged, causing the culprit to let out a yell or nearly jump out of his plow shoes with pain. One of the first cuss words I ever heard was when a jolted farmer yelled, "Jock, you old son-of-a-bitch!"

South of 154 highway on Main Street was the school lunchroom. Noon meals were served on a staggered schedule enabling different grades and high school students to be served a hot noon meal with food being provided by a federal surplus commodity program. There was the usual grumbling about the food but none was so severe as the month when prunes became the predominant menu item. Trainloads of prunes undoubtedly had been dried that season and most of them seemingly were shipped to Mullinville. The lunchroom cooks, all loyal hard working souls, went to all lengths to concoct any recipe using a preponderance of prunes. We were served stewed prunes, prune bread, and prune cake--we couldn't tell much difference between the two--prune butter and prune jam. Believe me, that month of prune brews eliminated any need for Ex-Lax.

Bernal Sayre's Grocery and Mercantile was the next door south of the lunchroom directly on Main Street. When school was on, any lucky kid with a nickel or dime could drop into Sayres' for a bottle of soda pop or a sack of red peanuts sprinkled with sweet, cinnamon-flavored Red Hots. What a delicious treat!

One day at noon, two or three brave kids each had a five-cent bet with Alan Ireland that he couldn't drink an entire bottle of soda pop without stopping or taking a breath. Alan prepared for the brave attempt by taking some deep breaths and flexing his Adam's apple. A big, cold bottle of Orange Kist was handed to Alan. He proceeded to begin glugging, as we watched spellbound, observing his eyes becoming watery and his Adam's apple bouncing up and down. To our amazement, he gulped down every last drop of the soda pop to win the bet. He received a standing ovation. Of course, all of us were already standing to get a closer view during the amazing feat.

My youngest sister, Doris, was very gregarious and outgoing. She enjoyed stopping by any business to say hello to the owner and to wish them a happy day. Bill Pilkington, Sayre's butcher, was a big, heavy guy always clad in a bloodstained white apron who worked behind the counter of the meat market. Doris had an unusual affinity toward bologna and would greet Bill the butcher with, "Bill, how is the bologna today?" Since she was one of his favorites, he would whack off a good chunk of the bologna with his long butcher knife, then reach across the top of the meat case and hand it to Doris, stuck on the point of his knife. Doris would enjoy the sample and thank him profusely for the treat, causing Bill to break into a broad, toothy grin.

Most of the kids in grade school wore gray canvas tennis shoes, mainly because they were the cheapest ones available. In the fall, my mama would call Sayre's and ask for Johnnie Kilgore, their shoe salesman. She would give Johnnie permission to fit me with a new pair of tennis shoes and put it on the charge account. I always liked Johnnie because he would ask me about life on Eagle Canyon Ranch or about my pony and dog. It turned out that he was born in the ranch house where his dad, William Kilgore, and his mother lived for a while when Mr. Kilgore was a carpenter during the construction of the ranch house in 1898.

South of Sayre's was the Mullinville telephone office. Telephone Brown kept the local phone lines singing, repairing breaks in the smooth wire after an ice storm or blizzard, or replacing large, green  glass insulators shot off by some distracted hunter. When we had ranch telephone outages, Mr. Brown would drive out to solve the problem. It was entertaining to watch him attach his steel spikes to his boots, securing them with a heavy leather strap around each leg. He then threw an even heavier leather strap around himself and the pole for safety. He would drive one spike into the wooden pole, then a second one, and lifting his foot each time, repeated the action as he walked himself up to the top of the pole. Standing on his spikes, he then leaned back on his waist strap to steady himself while he made the necessary repairs. Sometimes he would take a small box snapped to his belt that contained a telephone and wires with small clips on the ends. He attached the clips to the phone  lines and then talked to Mrs. Brown in town as he worked. She kept him informed of other service calls in the vicinity that he needed to remedy while he was out. I was really impressed by his actions. Mrs. Brown knew every phone number in Mullinville and the surrounding area by heart. She could listen in on any conversation, in addition to knowing who was going with whom, where, and when. Any subversive activity would soon be spread throughout the entire populace.

The U. S. Post Office was vital to the entire community, handling mail orders, parcel post deliveries, the newspaper, plus all first class mail. Even baby chicks were brought in by the Rock Island railroad and delivered to the post office for distribution. Papa would always drop in and tip his hat to Mrs. Bryan, the dedicated matronly lady and Post Mistress, to let her know how much she was appreciated. She always went the second mile to accommodate local citizens by opening up the window after church each Sunday, permitting customers to get their mail and the Sunday *Hutchinson News*. We could hardly wait to get home, change out of our Sunday clothes, and read the "funnies" printed in color in the paper. Some of our favorites were *The Katzenjammer Kids, Little Orphan Annie, Dick Tracy* and *Maggie and Jiggs*.

Hock Aldrich's Pool Hall, east of Nolan's Garage, was frequented by pool players who were smoking and betting money on their pool games. Papa didn't like the idea that fellows were loafing and not working and wouldn't let Kenny and me go there. We often moaned about not getting to learn to play pool.

The *Mullinville News* office was on the west side of Main, just south of the high school, which of course, was closed during the summer. Papa spent countless hours

Mullinville High School

at the school presiding over school board meetings in his forty-five years as president of the school board, beginning in 1919 and overseeing the construction of the new Mullinville Rural High School in 1925. Joe Cossell, editor of the *News*, was a close friend of Papa's, supporting him in each election bid starting in 1927 for the Kansas House of Representatives seat from the 93rd District. Myrtle Cossell, Joe's wife, was a Kansas Authors Club member along with Mama. Myrtle collected local news all week, then prepared it for the linotype operator to imprint the lead type which was then used in the press to print the newspaper. One of Jock Nolan's sons was their linotype operator. Cossell's only son, LaMont, occasionally filled in when needed.

Joe published the first XTRA edition of the *Mullinville News* with the headline, "JOY, JOY, It's a Boy!" printed in super bold type when Kenneth Benjamin arrived in January of 1922. He was the first boy to be born after three girls. The headline article read, "Ben Weaver was heard riding his mule through the canyons at Eagle Canyon Ranch shouting, "Joy, joy, It's a Boy!" Alas, when I arrived five years later, there was no special edition printed.

Cossell's small brindle bulldog named Boots, due to his four white feet, spent every working day at the news office. Toward noon each day, Joe would instruct Boots to "go get your lunch." They had made prior arrangements with the coffee shop, just west of Wright's Drugstore, to put a bone in a brown paper sack to await Boots' arrival. Boots would trot out the door and up Main Street, cross over the highway, and scratch on the back door of the coffee shop. Mary Gillette, the proprietor, was a hard-working, kindly lady supporting her badly crippled husband. She would invite Boots into the kitchen, fold down the top of the brown paper sack hiding his bone, thrust the folded sack top into his mouth, and then open the back door for his departure. Over the years, countless Mullinville residents enjoyed observing the obedient canine trotting back to the news office carrying his prize.

Bill Sager operated a large grocery store just north of the Co-Op elevator office. Bill was a heavy, friendly fellow and often used humor in his weekly grocery specials printed in the *Mullinville News*. One such example was foot-packed sauerkraut. It didn't seem to be very appetizing, but we laughed at the idea. We usually had an extra case of fresh eggs to exchange at Sager's for groceries. When Papa would hear of some neighbor having a struggle to keep food on their table, usually due to medical expense, he would get permission from Bill Sager to set up a food box and ask grocery patrons to purchase a few non-perishable items and drop them into the box. As a shopper approached, Papa would explain what a struggle the family was experiencing and appeal for a food donation. I contend Papa originated the concept of a food bank for the needy. When the box was filled, Papa delivered it to the family in need.

Numerous trips to Mullinville during the summer were similar yet different enough to make each one an exciting, new experience and gave me a greater appreciation of my hometown, Mullinville, Kansas.

No matter where life takes you,
don't forget where you came from.

CHAPTER SIX

Pigs in the Hudson

During my growing up years, my father tried to raise everything he could to feed our family and make a few dollars. It was crucial to economic survival during the hard times the country was facing in those days. The phrase "Use it up, wear it out, make it do or do without" was a household slogan along with "Waste not, want not."

Papa, like nearly every farmer, raised hogs since they would consume the household garbage, jackrabbits, unsalable grain, and various farm and garden vegetation. Bacon, hams, loins, sausage, and head cheese were all valuable supplements to the diet of rural families. We had plenty of skimmed milk left over after Blallen separated the cream from the milk and the cream was sold in town. When the sows farrowed, there was plenty of milk to feed the litters of baby piglets as they were weaned.

Hog butchering time was a big event. When the hogs were mature and fat, it was butchering time. Most families preferred to butcher in the late fall or early winter when the cooler weather made the hot, strenuous work more agreeable and when the

meat would keep better. The process required specialized equipment consisting of such items as a thirty gallon cast iron lard kettle, meat saws, meat grinders, sausage stuffers, and a tripod with block and tackle for lowering the slaughtered hog into the scalding vat of hot water.

Community butchering days were necessary due to the cost and amount of equipment required and gathering the able-bodied labor needed to get the work done in the shortest time possible. Earl Hammer, a big hog producer, had all the right equipment so neighbors hauled their porkers to his farm for the big event.

As a wide-eyed six-year-old, I always looked forward to the big day since the neighbor kids and I could run and play or swing on a tire hung under Earl's big mulberry tree. This kept us out of the way while the adults shared the hard labor.

The day started early and everyone had a part in the effort. Mortz Fromme brought his twenty-two caliber rifle. He plugged each hog between the eyes just before Earl rushed in with a huge butcher knife to slit the jugular vein and ensure thorough bleeding of the hog. Earl always caught some of the fresh warm blood in a tin cup and swigged it down before it clotted. Watching that bizarre act nearly caused us kids to erupt.

Once bled, a wood cross-arm was hooked between the rear leg tendons of the hog. The critter was hoisted up by block and tackle high enough to clear the vat of scalding water that was boiling over a hot, wood fire. The hog was lowered into the vat and kept in the scalding water until the hair slipped.

Next, the scalded hog was hoisted onto a big butchering table where the hog-bristle scraping crew removed all remaining hog hair from the skin. After the hog was gutted, a second crew with meat saws and sharp butchering knives quickly cut the carcass into side bacon, loin, picnic, and large hams. All back fat and excess ham fat was removed and tossed into a hot lard rendering kettle. It was melted down and poured into tin buckets to be used as cooking fat. Then the rendered lard and other pork products were divided equally among the neighbors who helped. They each had their own method of smoking and curing to preserve the meat when they got it home.

It seemed that there were so many chores to be done on the ranch that Papa was looking for a better or easier way to get our hogs butchered. Near butchering time the next fall, Papa saw an ad in the

Bucklin newspaper. It proclaimed that Slim Stout would provide a hog butchering, pork curing, and pork smoking service. That sounded like a good deal to Papa so he made an appointment for the next Saturday to deliver our hogs to Slim who lived about twenty miles from our ranch.

Saturday morning Papa and I hurried to the barn to load the hogs. Disaster! The old stock trailer was sitting there with a broken axle and flat tire. Papa didn't want to miss his appointment, so he decided the hogs had to be hauled in our big Hudson. He removed the rear seat cushion of the Hudson and lined the open car door up with the hog pen gate. Loading those three hundred pound porkers was quite a

chore for Papa and Blallen. They pushed, pulled, tugged, yelled, and grunted as they hoisted the stubborn critters up onto the back floor of the car.

By this time, the hogs were overheated so Papa rolled the back windows down halfway for ventilation. He slipped into the front seat of the car with me beside him. Papa instructed me, "Eldon, we're all set. You stand in the front seat by me. Hold this hammer by the handle and be ready to rap the snout of any hog that raises its head up over the backrest of the front seat." I gulped and sheepishly nodded, not sure if I was strong enough to control a three hundred pound hog with a rap on his snout.

We roared out of the barnyard and headed for Bucklin. All went well for a few miles with only the usual grunting and snorting of the overheated hogs. Suddenly a big squeal let us know a hog fight was starting. One big hog reared on his hind legs above the others and pushed his head over the backrest. Papa shouted, "Whap him hard on the snout."

I gave a mighty whack and that blow caused the angry hog to turn his head. As he turned, he spied the partly open window and gave a powerful lunge toward the opening. He shattered the glass which slit his throat as he sailed through the air and landed in the ditch. Before Papa could bring the Hudson to a screeching halt, the other two hogs followed. Both lunged through the broken window and were cut by the shards of glass still in the window frame. One hog was badly cut and bleeding profusely and the other broke a leg as he landed on the hard ground with his three hundred pound carcass. The loud squeals and awful wounds of the injured hogs were almost more than I could take.

Papa jumped out of the car, instructing me to remain inside while he ran to a nearby farmhouse to use their telephone. He frantically called the butcher. "Slim, I'm late. I've had an alarming disaster." Papa explained our terrible plight. Slim responded, "Ben, tell me where you are. I'll come right now with my truck and help you."

While waiting anxiously for Slim, Papa was forced to slash the throat of the first hog that had already gasped his last breath. Slim soon arrived in a cloud of dust and pulled his truck beside the dead and injured hogs. He reeled out a pair of barbed wire stretchers that were hooked to the front of the truck. With Papa heaving away and Slim pulling the stretcher rope, all three porkers were dragged from the roadside into the bed of Slim's truck. He drove full speed to Bucklin for the butchering.

Papa turned around at the next intersection and sped to the ranch house in our blood spattered Hudson reeking of hog manure. We stopped by the water hoses at the garage as Papa assured me, "With a good rinsing, we can clean up this mess on the floor and get rid of this sickening stench."

What he hadn't bargained for was that the horrible odor of hog manure had spread from the back of the Hudson and even permeated the front seat cushions and upholstery. He cut a piece of heavy cardboard and placed it in the missing back window to get the car ready for the drive to church the next morning.

The next morning Marjorie, Vivian, Doris, Kenny, Grandma Marriage, my parents, and I were dressed in our best outfits for the nine mile trip to church in Mullinville. In our home there was never a question of whether the family was going to church. It was just how we would all get there. Papa and Mama never missed a Sunday attending the United Brethren Church in Mullinville unless a blizzard snowed them in. Depending on the season, roads were either muddy and slick, full of ruts, dusty, or covered with snow drifts. The ordeal of getting to town was the major obstacle.

The eight of us crowded into the jump seats of the Hudson, all decked out in our Sunday best clothes. Papa had the hot water heater going full blast to help circulate the air and warm the car on that chilly morning. The car was soon filled with a strong hog manure odor. He sped up the road and seemed unable to hear Mama's and my sisters' repeated questions, "What is that horrible, sickening odor? It's just awful."

They complained and fussed all the way to town, repeating over and over, "We can't stand this smell. What is wrong? It's terrible!" No one was smiling, just complaining all the way. Later I heard Papa mumble, "Heavenly days, I've never seen such a carload of sour women!" Needless to say, the family car was never again used for hog hauling.

If you don't want anyone to find out about it, don't do it.

CHAPTER SEVEN

Catalpa Grove Jungle

A large green catalpa grove was growing vigorously in the canyon valley southeast of the ranch house. The trees were planted by Grandfather Marriage in the early 1900s when he learned catalpa trees grew straight and would make good fence posts. Although there was no creek running through the valley, every bit of rain running off the buffalo grass canyon banks gave the grove a good supply of moisture. The large catalpa leaves and overlapping branches of the dense growing trees made it appear as a jungle paradise to us kids. It provided a cooling shade from the hot sun and dry Kansas winds. Kenny, and his favorite cousin, Marilyn Marriage, were constant playmates since our Uncle Ira and his family lived on the ranch in a house about a mile from our ranch house. Kenny and Marilyn delighted in imagining they were Tarzan and his mate, Jane, in that jungle grove.

I was six years younger than the two of them, but sometimes they allowed me to tag along and play with them. I was labeled Chee-Chee, Tarzan's pet monkey. We used small branches and limbs from the trees to build a jungle house in the catalpa trees. This provided a hide-away in the dense foliage where no one could see us nor find us. Then we imagined how we could escape from lions or tigers who might be roaming in the jungle looking for a tasty meal.

Kenny and Marilyn were agile at swinging from the springy green branches and dared me to do the same. Each visit to our secret haven, I grew braver until I finally decided to attempt a risky swing through the branches. I chose a limb within reach, gave a mighty leap, and went crashing to the ground several feet below as the limb tore away from the tree trunk. Although dazed and unsure of my condition, a heavy bed of leaves broke my fall and I escaped without injury except to my pride. When Tarzan and his mate determined that I wasn't seriously hurt, they chided me relentlessly by saying, "No other monkey ever fell out of a tree!" This did teach me to learn to take "joshing" and not let my feelings be hurt.

As fall arrived, the slender green catalpa seed pods began turning dark as they ripened and became dry. L. J. Marriage, Marilyn's older brother, had taught Kenny how to smoke catalpa pods so he naturally had to teach us. Kenny was tall enough to reach the wooden matches in the match box on the kitchen wall and proceeded to light up our catalpa pod cigars. The pods were eight to ten inches long and it took a lot of suction to pull the smoke  through the narrow center of the pod. Although they tasted terribly bitter and burned our tender tongues, we felt pretty important at that moment, doing something we had seen grown-ups do and thinking this awful activity somehow made us more grown-up, too.

> Some think growing up is something that happens
> because you got older.
> But it turns out it's something you have to choose to do.

CHAPTER EIGHT

Green Tomato Pie

Cash was always mighty scarce so a variety of fund raisers were needed to support the county school system. Papa always reminded us that a silver dollar looked as big as a wagon wheel in those days. Box supper auctions were a popular way to raise money since everyone needed to eat. Ladies prepared their best recipes and provided an entire meal for two in a fancy, decorated box. Once sold in the auction, the buyer ate supper with the lady whose box he had purchased. The auctioneer was a real showman. Everyone listened to his chant and was excited about what each box would bring. He chanted long and loud to reach the highest possible price for each box, and joked as he reminded the men, "You don't have to eat with old Crabby tonight."

As president of the school board, Papa always attended the school events. At this particular event, Papa bid on a box for himself and then one for me. I was a pretty shy seven-year-old and wasn't hankering to eat with Sara, an old maid, whose box Papa had bought for me. Papa reminded me, "Now Eldon, show your good manners and help clean up all that fine food Sara has prepared so she won't be offended."

Sara knew about boys and asked me about my pony, Toots, and my dog, Tippy. Soon I was feeling more at ease. We got along great as I devoured the tasty pork tenderloin sandwiches and Kool-aid. Just as I was nearly filled up, Sara cheerfully announced, "I brought along my favorite homemade green tomato pie, just baked today." I gulped

 and swallowed hard 'cause I'd never tasted green tomatoes and nearly turned green imagining how terrible that pie was going to taste. I was feeling pretty peaked, to say the least.

Before I could say a thing, Sara served me a giant slice of pie and remarked, "There's plenty more for seconds, young man." There was no escape. My parents had always scolded us about never wasting food and eating what was put in front of us. So I made sure to have a big glass of Kool-aid handy in case I gagged and needed to wash down each bite.

Sara used several spices to jazz up the pie filling and it was much tastier than I ever imagined. I even ate a second piece. That experience taught me a good lesson. Never build up false fears or expectations about the unknown or reject an experience just because it is new. Instead, cultivate a "try it, you'll like attitude." Life's experiences, planned or spontaneous, can be more enjoyable that way.

> Look at everything as though you were seeing it
> either for the first or last time. ~Betty Smith

CHAPTER NINE

Mean Dog Episode

Papa loved people and our neighbors were always of special interest to him. I enjoyed tagging along with him on excursions to call on an ailing friend or simply inquire about the well-being of a neighbor. Sometimes we rode horseback across the green buffalo grass pastures; he on Old Roan and I on Toots, my bay half-Shetland. Toots was known as a "good-doer" and kept plump just on grass and a few whole oats. I learned to keep a tight cinch on my saddle or end up underneath her barrel-like sides.

While riding to a neighbor's, we always checked on the cows and calves as we crossed Eagle Lake pasture, in case any critter needed some medical treatments. Ailments could vary from a devil's claw around an old cow's pastern, or ankle, to a case of pink eye. Deciding how to handle the treatment and getting it done was always of source of excitement for me. I guess I felt important in helping my dad with these jobs.

This particular summer day we were going to call on old Mrs. Canfield, a lonely widow, and her bachelor son, Harvey. Papa had heard she was nearly bedfast suffering from consumption. It seems that when our country doctor, Doc Puckett, had trouble diagnosing a respiratory ailment, he labeled it consumption. The Canfield farm was a far piece down the road so we made the trip in the old '29

Chevy on that day. We always checked the oil first since it smoked quite a lot and we usually needed to add oil before driving it. Then, off we roared to the Canfield place.

Harvey saw us pull up at their farmstead and waved us toward the house. Papa killed the engine and we walked toward the kitchen door. Harvey opened the house door and announced that their dog didn't like strangers. Just as Papa reached for the screen door, a slinky mixed-breed dog appeared from nowhere, crept up behind us, and sank his teeth into the back of Papa's ankle just above the shoe. Papa never used a word of profanity in his life, but he did let out a sudden war whoop that scared the dog off and scared the living daylights out of me.

By now, blood was spurting out of the puncture holes in Papa's sock. Harvey opened the kitchen door and invited us in, then reached up on a shelf in the kitchen and brought down a bottle of turpentine. Harvey saturated the painful parts on Papa's ankle. He announced that they kept turpentine on the shelf above the kitchen door especially for dog bites. That remark made us wonder how many other visitors the old dog had bitten. Papa's visit with Mrs. Canfield was shorter than usual due to his aching ankle, although the stinging and burning from that fiery turpentine almost overshadowed the pain from the bite itself.

We stopped by Bill Collett's farm, Harvey's nearest neighbor, on the way back to the ranch to warn him about the Canfield's mean dog. However, we found that we were too late with our warning, as one of their boys had also been bitten by Old Slinky.

Less than a week later, we heard that Old Slinky had somehow been killed by coyotes. The truth finally came out, as it always does, when it was revealed that Mrs. Collett had been bitten by Old Slinky when she brought food in for the Canfield's. Her sons heard about that attack and that was the last straw. One dark night they disposed of Old Slinky and sent him to dog heaven, although Papa doubted Old Slinky would ever qualify.

In the meantime, Papa's ankle swelled up three times its normal size and Mama insisted he go to Doc Puckett. Doc said he might get blood poisoning. He gave Papa a tetanus shot and another powerful medication. Papa hobbled around for weeks before he was walking normally again.

I learned a valuable lesson that day when it comes to dealing with other people's critters and pets. Usually the barking dog won't bite, but always watch close for the quiet, slinky ones.

Once bitten, twice shy.

CHAPTER TEN

From Bad to Worse in the Dust Bowl Days

The terrible circumstances of the Great Depression took a turn for the worse in the plains states by the middle of the 1930s. Our area in western Kansas, eastern Colorado, and the panhandles of Oklahoma and Texas, were the hardest hit. A newspaper reporter of the time coined the term "dirty thirties" in describing the months of drought, high winds, and powdery dry soil that swirled up into violent clouds of dust sweeping across the central plains states. Minimum tillage and stubble-mulch farming was unheard of in those days. There were few native trees on the plains and no shelter belts to slow the strong wind's velocity.

The drought began in 1934 as the driest, hottest year on record. The lack of rainfall continued until the drought broke in 1939. Crops failed, native grasses died, and food for livestock was scarce. Plagues  of hungry grasshoppers and ravenous jackrabbits made the situation worse as they devoured every growing thing. Grasshoppers were reported to eat the wood off shovel handles and strip the leaves and bark from entire trees. The only things that would grow were weeds,

cockleburs, devil's claws, and prickly pear cactus. Gardens were scorched in the heat if not buried in the dust and food became scarce. Thousands of cattle and hogs were bought up by the government and slaughtered due to lack of grazing or forage. In some cases, the carcasses were buried in huge trenches even though people in areas of the country were going hungry. It was a terrible time of loss and hardship. People got by on hope, faith, and belief that someday it had to get better. It couldn't get any worse, it seemed.

The gigantic, billowing dust storms darkened the sun much like a huge storm cloud overhead. They were walls of blowing dirt that sometimes traveled as fast as sixty miles an hour. At times the storms came in so quickly that it became pitch dark in a matter of minutes. I can remember Mama lighting the kerosene lamps at mid-day during a summer dust storm which had darkened the entire house. The chickens went to roost thinking it was nightfall. Another time, a dust roller came in from the west as we were leaving a school program in town. We were lucky to be offered a bed for the night with one of our town friends. Everyone was warned it was too dangerous to drive in a dust roller. Just like a blinding snowstorm, the headlights on a car were too dim to light the road and keep the driver from running off into the ditch. If not injured by the car wreck, the occupants could be

lost in the dust and suffocate for lack of protection. Children were suffering from dust pneumonia and several hundred died of it during those years.

The gritty, powdery dust settled on everything. It was a constant battle to clean the house, furniture, beds, clothing, and cupboards after a particularly windy, all-day dust storm. Dust was in our eyes, throats, and even created a gritty sensation between our teeth. Fences and farm equipment were covered by three-foot diameter tumbleweeds, the dried remains of Russian thistle plants, that broke loose and tumbled across the flat land. When they were caught in fences, they soon trapped drifts of dust along miles of fence line. Cattle would walk over the fences on the drifts of dirt in search of forage.

The ranch house windows had to be left open for ventilation during the intense summer heat. That in turn invited sifting dust into the house. When we saw the billowing storms approaching, we all ran around the house, closing the huge casement windows to keep out as much dust as possible but it still sifted in through the gaps. Mama sometimes hung wet dish towels or wet pillowcases across the windows to help catch some of the dust particles and that produced a cooling effect inside the house as the water evaporated. As the wet

cloth dried, it became covered with a layer of mud that eventually turned into caked-on dirt.

As my folks did with my older brother, each school year started with a couple of new pairs of Big Smith overalls and a few new chambray shirts. All the grade school boys wore the same type of clothing. The overalls were one or two sizes too big for us at the start of school to allow for shrinkage of the overalls and for a growth spurt in each boy. We simply rolled up cuffs in each leg and gradually lowered the cuffs as we grew taller.

Girls wore dresses made from flour sacks, chicken feed sacks, inexpensive gingham, or calico. The flour and feed makers caught onto the idea and began using fabric prints in their sacks to improve sales. The girls' straight-cut dresses gave them room to grow, too. Mothers mended socks and sewed patches over holes in

clothes. There simply wasn't enough money to buy new clothes. So we wore what we had until the old ones were worn out or just too small and handed down to a younger child.

As children, we didn't realize how the years of poor crops and lack of income weighed on the shoulders of our parents. People seemed to be able to barter and trade to put food on the table and no one seemed to be going hungry. What we didn't realize was the seriousness of the worries plaguing our parents about money. For almost ten years, they worried about how to pay the mortgage on their land or how to pay off notes that had been taken out to buy seed for the next crop or to purchase calves to fatten. It was a time when many people finally gave up and moved on since there was no work and no way they could ever repay their debts. Our little town, like so many in Oklahoma and Kansas, dwindled in population. Nevertheless, the families that remained were determined to press on and expect better days. During those years, school activities, 4-H clubs, and numerous civic clubs were active. Remarkably, a library, city park, and a county historical society were founded during that dark decade.

We were all in the same situation. Everyone suffered a sense of loss during those times. We were convinced that if we had a nickel for every time we heard the advice, "Use it up, wear it out, make it do or do without" we would be millionaires.

The happiest people don't worry too much about whether life is fair or not, they just get on with it. ~Andrew Matthews

CHAPTER ELEVEN

Cyclone Catastrophe

The year I completed first grade was the same year Marjorie graduated from college. It was a joy for Mama and Papa to have her home for the summer. She had a college boyfriend and was excited about teaching school in Valley Center until he would graduate the following year. She had a beautiful voice and majored in English and voice in college. Vivian talked to Marjorie a lot about college that summer as she was preparing to attend the same school, Kansas State Teacher's College, in the fall.

I was a blue-eyed tow-head and they all thought I was the cutest little brother. My sisters doted on me and gave me a lot of hugs and kisses. It made me feel special to get so much attention, but sometimes I begged my mother to make the girls stop kissing on me. We loved having family talent nights when Marjorie was home and she played the old Elburn piano. Papa and Mama were able to have more time to attend meetings and events in town when my sisters were out of school for the summer. One such day, they were in town for a school board meeting. Marj was in charge and all of us were at home, including Grandma Marriage. We had one of the most frightening experiences that evening that I could ever remember. Marj wrote about the entire episode to her fiancé, Jerome Carroll.

Cyclone Catastrophe

Sunday August 26, 1934.

"Well, Sweetest, I came as near to being killed as I ever want to be last Monday night. We had a terrible cyclone here and our place is really an awful wreck. About eight o'clock in the evening, the lightning and thunder started and just popped around pretty lively. Then an awful dirt storm came up and it got pitch dark.

We were eating supper or trying to. We were all pretty nervous but were trying to keep Eldon from being afraid. The storm came from the northeast. About eight-thirty, the wind started to get worse and from then until nine o'clock, I expected the house to go over into the canyon at any minute.

It was awful! The screen porch on the house was ripped clear off. Dad's cherry tree snapped off, the summer house made into kindling wood, the garage completely torn down, and the roof fell on Grandma's car and pushed it about thirty feet backwards. The radiator was ruined. Now the walls of the garage are all flat on the ground.

It bent the windmill clear over double and blew the wheel and tower over in a canyon. The barns were moved off their foundations and the roofs badly torn up. The corral was blown all to pieces. Worst of all, the big cattle shed north of the house was completely demolished. Not one bit of it was left. Dad's horse, Buck, was in the shed and we found him the next day, not hurt at all but wrapped up in wire. How he escaped I don't know.

Windows on all four sides of the house were blown in and the rain just poured in. The big window by the piano in the parlor crashed in and the water nearly ruined the piano. I was just sick but we could do nothing. The rain came in all over the roof as the wind had torn off the shingles over it. Then, the kitchen door glass broke out and a west window and by that time there was such a wind through that we expected the roof or house to go any time.

We started to dash for the basement once, but lightening showed us that all the banisters and railings were gone and the wind was so bad we knew we couldn't make it so we had to stay in. I was awfully brave really because Eldon and Kenneth were both terribly frightened and I knew I couldn't give way. Grandma wasn't much help. Every time a window would crash in she'd blow out the light thinking the house was going and I'd have to fight off two or three kids so I could get it lighted again. Never again do I want to live through such a half hour. I doubt if I'll ever have to, however.

Mother and Dad came driving in about ten o'clock and they were awfully scared. The phone line had been torn down and they didn't know what had happened. It seems as if we've had about enough bad luck. Dad was clear down with the blues or heartache the next day. But he's feeling better now because we had a two inch rain with it and we had a little insurance. The windmill couldn't be insured so it's a total loss. My nerves are still a little on edge."

For months afterwards, whenever a dust roller or dark thunderstorm was brewing on the horizon, I recalled that evening. It was a powerful cyclone that destroyed nearly everything in its path but somehow the ranch house and our family were spared. Memories of the howling wind, lightening, driving rain, and crashing windows came back to me. Kenny and I shrieking in the dark when the lamp went out was probably the scariest memory for me as a seven-year-old boy. The next day we surveyed the twisted wreckage of the windmill, damaged barns, and the pitiful pile of splintered boards and  lumber that remained from our massive cattle shed. It was several days before Papa found a dead horse in the wreckage of the shed. There was a two by four board in his skull driven by the powerful winds. Papa and Mama shook their heads in disbelief at the amount of damage. "That was a close call," was all that Papa could say as he thought about our family surviving the storm. The extensive damage was a devastating loss at a time when we had already suffered several years of low prices, poor yields, and almost no income. Without complaining and simply being thankful the family was safe, Mama and Papa picked up the pieces. Their faith helped us to cope with the dust storms, cyclones, fires, and other near catastrophes. There wasn't much we could do but pick ourselves up, dust off, and go on with life.

Things can be replaced; people can't.

CHAPTER TWELVE

The Day Time Stood Still

Cold cash or spending money was as scarce as rain in Kansas as I grew older. It was especially hard for an eight-year-old boy to earn any spending money. It was lucky for me that mice were plentiful and easily invaded the four-story ranch house. Mama hated the dreaded creatures and offered me a penny for each trapped mouse. Traps and bait were already available so I was soon in business. It was a real challenge to try to outsmart the pesky rascals. Bacon and yellow cheese were the most tempting bait to entice the mice to nibble and snap the trap trigger.

Some crafty critters could steal the bacon without tripping the trap, so I learned the tedious task of tying bait on the trap tongue using sewing thread. Fall and winter were the best trapping seasons as cold weather drove pests to hunt for warmer surroundings. On a good night, I trapped four to six mice. In some of the darker, less occupied storage rooms of the ranch house, the mice frolicked about more freely so I ran my traps twice a day. The pennies began to fatten up my piggy bank but not fast enough.

Fly swatting income arrived with warm weather. Even with screen doors, flies were a perpetual nuisance. Mama offered me a penny for every twenty-five flies I killed. The screen wire swatter with a long handle was sure death to one of those pests; nailing three flies with a single swat was my record. It was still a slow procedure to add up to twenty-five dead flies.

One evening while gathering eggs in the hen house, I noticed solid swarms of flies on the edges of the water trough--what an opportunity! I could hardly gather the eggs fast enough and rush to the house for the trusty fly swatter. Back at the hen house my first swat netted fourteen flies. I could just imagine those pennies rolling in. I soon had over two hundred dead flies worth eight cents.

When I dashed to the house to collect my reward, my excitement turned to despair. Mama immediately recognized the smaller barn or livestock flies and made it clear she paid only for houseflies. My golden bubble had burst but I still had plenty of ornery houseflies to stalk. I simply had to spend much more time to accumulate those pennies.

Papa always carried a work pocket watch on a silver chain in the pocket of his Big Smith overalls. He'd pull out his watch about noon to check the time before heading to the ranch house for a hearty dinner. Watching this action gave me a burning desire to have my very own pocket watch. I looked up watches in the big Montgomery Ward or "Monkey" Ward catalog. There was a shiny one with a second-hand and an MW emblem on the face for one dollar and twenty-seven cents and guaranteed for ninety days. That did it! I had to have a watch that I could carry in my Big Smith overall watch pocket just like Papa did with his watch. It took me several months as an eight-year-old to save the dollar and twenty-seven cents required to order that prized watch.

Every spare minute when I wasn't gathering eggs, feeding chickens, or helping milk the cows, I was trapping and swatting. Finally, the big day came. My watch was ordered along with the household supplies order which saved me paying postage. Once the order was mailed, the days seemed to drag by waiting for the package from Ward's.

Riding everyday on my pony, Toots, she'd gallop the half-mile to the mailbox. I was so hoping the shipment had arrived. Finally, the great day! Toots raced me home as fast as she could. I tied her reins to the hitching bar, ran into the house, and ripped open the package to admire my shiny pocket watch. What a beauty!

After reading all the instructions, I wound and set it and was immediately intrigued by the little second hand clicking away. Papa reminded me it would be easy to lose my watch out of my overalls pocket so he suggested tying it on a string to secure it from loss. I carried it securely tied to a black shoestring in my overall watch pocket.

From then on, I felt mighty important whipping out my shiny MW watch to remind Papa it was time to head home for dinner. My penny-saving had paid off.

All went well for a few days until I tossed my dirty overalls in the laundry hamper. About noon that day, I reached for my watch in my overalls and the pocket was empty! My heart sank. The house rule was to empty all pockets before throwing dirty clothes in the hamper. I knew it was wash day and I had been reminded by Mama to always empty my overalls pockets before putting them in the clothes hamper. Papa called out, "Dinner time," and we headed for the ranch house.

One of Blallen's least desirable duties was pumping the hand-driven Dexter wood-framed, galvanized tub washing machine. Not only was it hard work for the entire day, but it kept him from his favorite chore of driving the tractor. The washday chore involved carrying gallons of boiling hot water, scrubbing stains with lye soap, and lifting wet clothes from the washer tub to the wringer. Then the clothes had to be carried to the lower courtyard of the ranch house to be hung on the clothes line to dry.

I dashed down the stairs to the laundry room where Blallen was pumping the handle of the old washing machine. Blallen pushed and pulled the wooden washer handle which pumped the plunger up and down in the hand operated washer full of soapy, hot water. I was too late! He'd already washed the overalls. When he began cranking clothes through the wringer, he discovered my watch. He presented it to me, dangling from the shoestring, oozing with water and soap bubbles from under the glass crystal. Bad news for watches.

My heart sank thinking that was the end of time. I was heartbroken and began to sob, feeling certain my most prized possession was completely ruined. When washday was finished, Bill felt sorry for me and came to the rescue. He popped off the back of my watch with his trusty pocket knife, blew all the water and suds out of the works, dunked it into a can of kerosene, and hung it up by the shoestring to dry.

After the back was replaced, I set the time and wound the watch. I was elated when it started ticking off the seconds. It ran like a Singer sewing machine and I was overjoyed to have it in running order. What a relief to gain many more months of timekeeping from my adored Monkey Ward watch. Another valuable lesson was learned about working hard to earn spending money, taking care of my possessions, and following the instructions and advice of my mama.

Good judgment comes from experience.
Experience is the name we give our mistakes.

CHAPTER THIRTEEN

A Boy's Best Friends

I could hardly wait to come home from school and be greeted by Dick, the Eagle Canyon Ranch dog. He was my constant companion and guardian from the time I was toddler and just learning to walk. Dick was a black and sable shepherd-collie mix with a natural herding instinct. His short, pointed ears stood up on his head and fluffy whiskers jutted out from his face. He looked smart and alert despite having the wiry, scruffy coat of a ranch dog. Dick kept me herded away from danger such as falling off a canyon bank or encountering a venomous rattlesnake when I played with my toys in the yard near our house.

Anytime Papa saddled a horse to do chores around the ranch, Dick was right at his side to keep Papa company. As Papa galloped across the pastures and canyons, Dick raced happily along beside Old Roan and Papa.

One afternoon, the old oak wall telephone jingled three longs and a short, the telephone number for Eagle Canyon Ranch. Mama answered and the neighbor calling asked for Ben Weaver. She called Papa to the telephone. He recognized the voice of Art Lutz on the line reporting that old Major, our aged Marriage Mulley bull, had broken through the five-strand barbed wire fence into their cow pasture. The excited and upset Lutz brothers wanted the old bull out of there right away. They didn't want their big bull or cows mixing with old Major.

The term Mulley describes a polled, or hornless, breed of cattle developed by my grandfather, John Marriage. They were a dual purpose breed, large and deep red in color, without a white spot. Grandfather selected Eagle Canyon Ranch in the late 1890s as a range area to propagate the popular breed he had developed. Characteristic of his breeding, Major was a powerfully muscled, deep red sire weighing over two thousand pounds and Papa knew he would be a handful to drive back to Eagle Canyon Ranch from the Lutz place.

Following the telephone call, Papa said to Mama, "I have to get right over there. Those Lutz boys are wound up tighter than a pocket watch over this bull situation." Papa hustled to the horse barn to saddle Old Roan, his favorite iron-gray stock horse. He looped a blacksnake whip around the saddle horn as he prepared to leave for the Lutz cow pasture. I begged to ride along on my pony, Toots, but Papa warned me this chore was far too dangerous for a seven-year-old to come along. The Lutz bull was heavily horned and known for being easily roused into a raging charge. Papa related that if the two powerful bulls ever encountered each other in the huge pasture, separating them would be difficult and dangerous. Yet, it had to be done to keep Major from being injured by the Lutz horned bull.

When Papa reached the Lutz pasture, he left the barbed wire gate open wide since he planned to drive Major through it upon their return. Papa could see the dust flying in the distance and soon heard the commotion, pawing, bellowing, and snorting of the two huge bulls as they began fighting for dominance in the pasture.

Papa coaxed Old Roan into a hard gallop with Dick at their heels and began whooping and hollering as he neared the angry bulls. Papa lashed out twice across Major's broad back with the blacksnake. The distraction from his yelling, coupled with the loud, sharp crack of the whip temporarily broke up the skirmish. Suddenly, the maddened, horned Lutz bull wheeled, gave a loud bellow, and with head down charged directly toward Papa. Old Roan gave a snort and froze dead in her tracks, leaving Papa helpless to escape the charging bull.

Faithful Dick, who instinctively sensed the danger of his master's situation, dashed directly into the melee and sank his teeth into the bull's tender nose, breaking the charge.

The bull threw his huge head violently from side to side trying to shake Dick loose to stop the pain caused by Dick's clenched teeth in his nose. In doing so, the bull swung Dick's entire body back and forth and eventually the bull gored Dick in the side with his horn. Once Dick released his grip, the snorting, bloody-nosed bull trotted away to lick his wound. Meanwhile, Major roamed back through the open gate to Eagle Canyon Ranch.

Papa quickly dismounted, gathered Dick in his arms, and carried him to the nearest county road. A sheep truck driver heading for Mullinville stopped to lend assistance. They carefully laid Dick on an old coat on the floorboard of the truck and roared on toward the veterinarian. Doc Puckett was home and while sewing up the dog's gaping wounds, listened as Papa related the life-saving story of Dick's heroism.

Doc painted a gloomy picture for Dick's recovery due to the severe blood loss and possible internal injuries. He suggested Dick would have the best chance for survival undisturbed at home in familiar surroundings. Once back at the ranch house, Papa spread a heavy blanket on the back porch where Dick always enjoyed napping and probably dreamed he was chasing jackrabbits. Dick slept most of the next two days rousing only to lap some cool water but he would eat nothing. The second night, he passed on to dog heaven, having given his all to save his master.

Our entire family and ranch hands were saddened by Dick's death. He was a faithful, devoted companion in life and a brave, heroic champion in death. Dick received a reverent, suitable burial on the canyon bank where he often basked in the sunshine near the Marriage Mulley cows he so fondly tended. Papa sent a short obituary to the newspaper in memory of our beloved dog who saved his life.

It was heartbreaking for me when Dick died. He was the most faithful pet I had known and was my constant companion for seven years. I couldn't imagine how I could live without my best friend. Papa knew how sad and lonesome I was for my dog, so he soon found a neighbor who was trying to give away puppies to a good home.

Soon I had a new companion. Tippy, a terrier mix, so named due to the white tip on his tail, was mottled black and white with sharp ears and a smiley face. He loved to wrestle, jump, and chase me around the buffalo grass area in front of the ranch house. Tippy would retrieve a small rubber ball or a stick thrown in his direction which delighted me and  kept both of us entertained. He went with me as I played around the ranch, went to the barn, and helped with ranch chores. He was just small enough to be allowed in the house as an inside dog, despite being a ranch dog. Papa and Mama laughed at the sight of the menagerie that could be seen loping across the ranch with me on Toots, followed by her colt, and trailed by little Tippy who tagged along at a trot.

In the hot, dry summer, I slept on the back porch situated on the east side of the ranch house. There was usually a refreshing breeze blowing at the end of a hot summer day. Tippy's favorite trick was to  jump up on my bed in the mornings while I was still sleeping, slip under the quilt beside me, and take a nap. He snuggled close to me with only his head peeking out next to my chin. One such morning, Mama crept up to the bedside with her Kodak box camera and took our photograph. She thought it was such an endearing pose that she sent it to a farm magazine and received a year's free subscription when they published the photograph. We were all proud of that honor.

One sunny morning, Tippy failed to wake me. His absence really worried me, so I quickly slipped on my blue and grey striped Big Smith overalls and began running around the ranch house. I looked everywhere as I called his name, but heard no barking in response. I dashed up the hill toward the barn calling even louder for my beloved Tippy. Blallen was busy milking the cows and declared he hadn't seen Tippy that morning. By this time, I was terribly worried about what had become of him. I bridled my roly-poly pony, Toots, jumped on her back and rode around the nearby canyons shouting for Tippy. My thought was that he might have been chasing a jack rabbit and followed the rabbit into a hole where he might be trapped and couldn't get out.

All of my searching and calling for Tippy was in vain and there was no sign or response from him. No one in the family had seen him. Blallen was carrying the milk back to the house when I returned from my search. His comment was, "I reckon that some hungry mother coyote could have grabbed Tippy and carried him back to her den to feed her pups." Then I began to wonder if a hawk or eagle had grabbed Tippy with its talons and carried him off. That thought really made me feel extra lonely, sad, and worried about my special little dog. Papa tried to console me and promised I could have another dog if Tippy never came home. Sadly, he didn't.

I was elated that a neighbor, Charley Burrton, owned a dog with a new litter of puppies and offered me the pick of the litter. I was filled with anticipation as we climbed into the old blue 1929 Chevy and whizzed over to the Burrton farm. As we drove along, Papa mentioned to me that Mrs. Burrton was famous for her delicious fried chicken. All their chickens roamed and foraged for bugs, seeds, and tender grass as free range chickens but they were too wiry and wild to catch. As a result, when Mrs. Burrton needed some fryers, Charley would take his shotgun and blow off a few heads.

Charley's puppies were a delightful sight to behold. I knelt down and began to pet and play with them. I felt so special to be allowed to choose my favorite puppy from seven fat and cuddly soft bundles of fur. When one very alert, bright-eyed puppy happily licked my hand, that was it. He was my pick. He was white with sorrel spots. I named him King after the great dog, Yukon King, of the Royal Canadian Mounted Police radio program that I loved to listen to on our radio.

King quickly grew and adjusted to ranch life as he followed me into the cow barn when we were milking. He happily lapped up warm milk that I poured into the barn cats' pan. I chased the cats and kept them at bay until King had his fill. One fun stunt King learned was to sit on my red wagon while I pulled it at top speed around the yard at the ranch house. Now I had another dog and a playmate. Owning an array of dogs in my growing up years made life much more fun and entertaining. It was amazing to me how forgiving a dog could be, even after being scolded for misbehaving. They were always cheerful and welcoming even after just a short time apart. Truly, dogs were a boy's best friend, adding greater joy and happiness to the life of a growing boy.

A dog's sole purpose in life is to give his heart to his master.

CHAPTER FOURTEEN

City Cousins' Ranch Reunion

The first of several exciting summer visits of my city cousins to Eagle Canyon Ranch, as nearly as I can recollect, was in 1936 when I was nine years old. The way this annual tradition came about requires some explanation to truly appreciate its importance.

My dad, Benjamin Opdyke Weaver, was called Pop, by us five Weaver children. Pop was shortened from Papa by my sister who thought Pop was more up-to-date. He was the oldest son in a family of eleven children. Pop had several brothers and bunches of sisters, all of whom Grandfather Weaver believed should have an education. This was quite unusual for young women in those days. He saw to it that Pop's sisters each received college training at Friends University in Wichita, Kansas. This put them in a position to either support themselves or to meet and marry educated men. Eventually, his sisters each married professional career men who mostly were employed in towns or cities rather than working on a ranch or farm in a rural area. Thus, I had several city cousins.

Despite Pop's siblings being educated, the hard times of the Depression continued to create financial hardships. Even the men who still had jobs were strapped for cash and faced high prices for food, clothes and other necessities. There was never any money left over for vacations, movies, favorite toys, or candy. There were no summer sports or recreation programs and children with long days of idle time without supervision in the city spelled trouble. The popular activity for city boys after dusk was to roam the streets in gangs and steal items from flashy cars that were produced during the 1930s. Shiny chrome hub caps, fancy hood ornaments, and illuminated front fender guides were considered a trophy when stolen from these vehicles. There was usually an older boy or unemployed young man who bought and sold the stolen items which provided a little spending money for city boys who had nothing to do. Too much free time also offered the boys entirely too much opportunity to fraternize with the neighborhood girls, which proper young men in those days shouldn't be found doing.

With these fears and pitfalls in mind, my aunts who lived in Wichita and Topeka organized a campaign to coerce Pop into taking their boys to Eagle Canyon Ranch to spend the summer. Aunt Beth's plea was, "Benny, just think of how healthful that fresh air and sunshine would be for the boys." Other aunties helped build their case by telling Pop, "Just think of how much work you can get out of these fine boys."

Pop knew they were just whistling Dixie because he had previously been exposed to boys' antics while he was a teacher in his early twenties. When he originally arrived at Eagle Canyon Ranch in 1912, he was employed by Grandfather Marriage to teach at Sunflower School and oversee a group of orphan boys from Topeka. When it came to getting work out of those orphan boys from the city, Pop used to say, "One boy equals a boy, two boys are half a boy, and three boys are no boys at all." Another of Pop's beliefs was, "Idle hands spell trouble." He joked that he never heard of a fatality among boys due to overwork. Experience and better judgment aside, Pop and Mama would never refuse to help someone when there was a need, so they agreed to the idea. They most likely realized the best way to keep the city cousins out of trouble was to get them out of the city and away from temptations.

After much discussion and planning, it was decided that my city cousins would begin arriving around the first of June that summer. I was overjoyed as a nine-year-old who never knew what it was like to have after-school playmates nearby let alone all summer long. My sisters treated me royally, but they weren't interested in my games of mumble-peg, marble shooting, BB guns, or top spinning. For the most part, Kenny considered me a nuisance and little pest. At fourteen, he had more important interests in working for other ranchers, his town friends, girls, and cars. Spending time with him was a rarity, if ever. Therefore, as the cousins began arriving, I pictured them as constant playmates and began thinking of endless ways to enjoy those hot, summer days with them.

The Wichita cousins, Ernie Reiger, and his younger brother, Bobbie, were the first to arrive. Aunt Bertie and her boys, Bill and Elmer Rusco, were already living with us at the ranch. Bill Weaver of Topeka soon joined the group. Last, and not least, was Jack Clevenger, who was not a cousin, but a next door neighbor to Grandfather Weaver, who lived in Wichita at that time. Mrs. Clevenger, a French widow, pleaded with Grandfather and Pop to take Jack away from the Wichita gang influences. We were a rather motley crew, ranging in age from Bobby Reiger, who was seven, to Jack Clevenger who was fourteen. Ernie, Bill

Eldon & Woolo

Weaver and I were nine and Elmer was eight. There seemed to be a natural pecking order among us based on our ages and personalities.

We all enjoyed Jack because he had an extroverted, entertaining personality and always livened up the situations in which we found

ourselves. He was husky and tall and much stronger than the younger boys. Living in the city, he was street-wise and knew about the gangs of boys who stole from cars, smoked cigarettes, and had other bad habits that were banned at the ranch. Jack seemed brave and bragged about his ability to ride any horse or try anything. As the oldest boy, he was usually the instigator of pranks and jokes. We loved learning songs from him as he had a good voice and loved to sing. *Dunderback*

Pete & Blallen

Jack Clevenger

was soon one of our favorite songs as we did chores together around the ranch.

Ernie and Bobby Reiger were true city slickers to me. Their father, Herbert, who was a pharmacist, operated a drug store and soda fountain. Ernie, a chunky, full-faced boy was my age. He had a big appetite but was not so eager to do ranch chores and hard work. It seemed he enjoyed lazing around his father's drug store, eating ice cream, and not doing much of anything. However, he was an amiable lad and normally we weren't too upset with him when he shirked his share of the chores. During the summer, I overheard Pop chuckle as he told Mama, "I don't think that Ernie will ever amount to anything, but we must do our best to guide him." Bobby was the youngest of our crew. He was fun-loving, happy, and always easy to get along with when we played or did our chores.

Bill Rusco, also known as Woolo, due to his short, curly brown hair, was slender and slightly built. He was more introverted and shy than most of the Weaver family but he was a good worker. No doubt he was affected by his father's death and somewhat less confident than the other cousins. He was a brilliant boy with not much common sense. My mother, his Aunt Etta, engaged him in lengthy conversations to promote and stimulate his already vast knowledge, particularly about science. She bought him a science kit so he could do experiments. He always seemed to be concocting some type of mixture or potion to see what would happen.

Elmer, nicknamed Peter Rabbit, was Bill's younger brother and similar in personality and looks to Bill. He had straight brown hair and being closer to my age, we thought of each other as best friends. My mother took to calling us the twins since we dressed alike, spent so much time together, and enjoyed the same activities.

Bill Weaver came from Topeka where my uncle, Ernest "Buck" Weaver, was a coach and teacher at Topeka High School. Bill was taller than the rest of us near his age and more stoutly built. He was friendly and easy-going which made him one of my favorites, too. And Pop liked the way Bill cooperated and complied with whatever we boys were asked to do. It was clear that my uncle applied his coaching and teaching discipline at home, too.

With seven boys of our ages descending upon the ranch like flies on honey, Pop always needed help to oversee our crew, keep us in line, and generally make sure none of us were lost, injured, or into too much mischief during the long, hot summer days. It required a lot of effort to keep seven boys busy in hopes we would be too exhausted to cause much trouble. Blallen was usually around to keep an eye on us, but more help was needed. Pop assigned the job of foreman to Warren Marriage of Colorado Springs. He was the son of Mama's first cousin, Russell, making Warren my second cousin.

His parents, Kathleen and Russell Marriage, were busy in the summer with their Upton Gardens nursery and, similar to the other Weaver cousins, the ranch was a perfect place to send him to keep him out of trouble. Warren was sixteen and we thought he hated leaving his bosom buddies, girlfriends, and the cool, clear mountain air of Colorado to end up in hot, dirty Kansas doing ranch work. When he first arrived at the ranch, it didn't seem that he was in the most joyous frame of mind. We were convinced he took out his resentment on us. Privately, we referred to him as a slave driver who made us endure long periods of hard work without even a glug of water from our communal gallon water jug.

In time, Dux was the nickname given to Warren because of his response to all the new and exciting things he was seeing and experiencing daily at our home. He would often shriek with joy, "Oh, isn't that just ducky!" He became totally enthralled and full of exuberance at being with our large, happy family. So, we began calling him Ducky and later shortened his nickname to Dux. He seemed to love the new-found moniker and responded to it with pride.

We were especially fond of hiking in the canyons, playing in the catalpa grove, and riding horses. Blallen found some old wagon wheel hubs and removed the metal hoops for us. Then, he taught us about hoop rolling which was a game he enjoyed as a child. We each used a lathe stick to roll the metal hoops around the yard, learning how to

give the hoop a whack with the stick to keep it rolling in the direction we wanted it to go.

The remains of an old well that was south of the pond fascinated us. It had caved in and filled with dirt over the years, and a lone cottonwood tree once grew there. Local legends persisted that it was a stopping point along a freight line that ran from Kinsley to Fort Supply during the late 1800s. The well once was large enough to water teams of horses. We had found a few signs that a barn or corral once stood nearby. A few shallow wagon ruts in the vicinity could be seen in the hard, dry clay. Doris remembered wild stories that Uncle Ralph had told and she in turn, told to us. She had a great imagination and could frighten and astound us with stories about Cheyenne and Arapaho Indians fighting with the U. S. Calvary who tried to protect the early settlers in the Cherokee Outlet. And for us boys, the snakes that infested the well really attracted our attention. We soon found that Ernie was entranced by snakes.

Our ranch chores consisted of helping Blallen with the milking and hoeing prickly pear cactus that plagued the grama grass pastures around the ranch. Dry, hot sunny days caused the cacti to spread, even killing out the hardy native buffalo grass. The thriving cacti  created an opportune situation to keep boys occupied through chopping and hoeing the pesky succulents. Hoeing and milking chores were never ending, so Pop knew he would always have something to keep our gang of seven busy. Blallen never seemed to have much patience for us and could be heard grumbling about our antics. The boys would beg Blallen to relate his experiences from World War One when he served in France. All they were able to get him to say was a poem about the German Kaiser Wilhelm, also known to the Allied troops as Kaiser Bill. Blallen recited the words in his gruff but sing-song fashion. "Kaiser Bill went up the hill, to take a shot at France. Kaiser Bill ran down the hill, with bullets in his pants!" We all had a good laugh imagining a young Blallen with a rifle chasing Kaiser Bill.

After a day of work, we headed to the big cattle and horse watering tank near the ranch house and happily leaped stark naked into the tank for a cool swim and bath. After supper, some of us slept on top of the summer house. It was a large gazebo-type structure constructed of lathe and covered with ivy. A table with benches on each side was shaded by the summer house where we could eat in the yard near the house. A mattress and wire bed springs sat on the roof of the gazebo where we climbed up to go to sleep.

Otherwise, we slept in the boy's room, which was a large bunk house room next to the house. It had been used to bunk cowboys and single hired men from the late 1890s and up into the early 1920s.

When the cousins invaded Eagle Canyon Ranch for the summer, it created an additional load on the kitchen crew of my three sisters, Marjorie, Vivian, and Doris. Vivian was a Home Economics major at Kansas State Teacher's College and an authority on entertaining, table settings, and table manners. Vivian was appalled at some of the atrocious table manners of some of the city cousins. She remarked to Mama that the boys needed some lessons on manners and how to properly set a table. Mama knew the girls were outnumbered and could certainly use some extra help. From that day on, the boys were periodically assigned to set the dining table under Vivian's guidance and instruction. As rambunctious, hungry grade school boys, we couldn't understand all the fuss about table manners.

Vivian gave us directions forcefully, yet tactfully. Silverware was to be placed one inch from the edge of the table, with forks to be placed on either side of the dinner fork in the order of use, water glasses at the knife point, and coffee cup beyond the forks. It all had to be done to her standards before the family and other ranch hands arrived for dinner.

Vivian gave us instructions on holding our silverware properly. There were absolutely no baby-fist grabs on the folk or spoon, and each boy learned to use the proper hands to grasp the knife and fork when cutting meat. There was to be no more talking with food in one's mouth. And napkins, rather than shirt sleeves, were to be used to wipe our faces. She was a forceful instructor, making a strong impression on all of us, well remembered from that day forward.

Pop, Blallen, and Dux kept the rambunctious gang busy and we never ran out of cactus to hoe or things to do. It seemed like all the cousins were having a good time and enjoying a sense of freedom by being away from their parents. Somehow they knew they had to behave and obey Pop's rules or be in bigger trouble back home. It was the best summer I could remember. Despite the heat, dust, and sun, it didn't really seem like work when we were rewarded with a cool swim, free time to play, and then a hearty supper.

Every boy should know how to work hard
by the time he becomes a man.

CHAPTER FIFTEEN

Ernie and the Hog Wallow Plot

The first week of cactus detail was the toughest as we adjusted to the one hundred degree sun, dust, and scorching wind. We dressed as sparingly as possible by wearing bib overalls to protect our legs and ankles, and work boots. Even shirts and caps were avoided in our desire to overcome the heat. Cousin Ernie soon discovered he could feign a headache or heat stroke and persuade our foreman of the cactus detail, Dux, to let him lie in the shade under the old '29 Chevy to recuperate. The old Chevy transported us to the pasture as we perched on front fenders, running boards, and the interior seats. Dux was a wild driver causing us to hang on for dear life as he roared up and down canyons to the big Eagle Lake pasture that was highly infested by prickly pear cactus. The years of drought had practically killed all the native grasses so Pop's solution to beat the cactus was our hoeing crew of seven.

Each day, Dux would map out the area of cactus to be demolished before we could sail back to the ranch house and happily leap stark naked into the big horse tank for a cool swim and bath. It wasn't long before we figured out that while Ernie was napping in the shade, we were hoeing his cactus, causing us more blisters and a longer day in the hot sun. Jack Clevenger started the rumblings and a conspiracy to cure Ernie of feigning exhaustion or goofing off. Jack had grown up street-wise in Wichita and being the oldest, tended to influence our behavior. We all knew Pop wouldn't tolerate any form of physical violence that would injure anyone. Consequently, beating up Ernie wasn't the solution. Suddenly, Jack had an inspiration. "We'll all gang up on big, lazy Ernie and heave him, clothes and all, into the black, slimy, stinky hog wallow. That should cure him of his goofing off."

Jack contended that plopping Ernie face down into the hog wallow wouldn't really hurt him but would teach him a lesson he would never forget. By this time of the summer, water overflowing the horse tank had created a sea of mud where fat hogs and sows wallowed to cool off. The stagnant muck was about two feet deep and intermingled with hog manure causing a strong stench. It was the least desirable place for any human. Jack had us all sworn to secrecy, realizing Ernie was big and heavy, and it would require a surprise

attack and united effort to down him. Toward sundown, Jack reminded us all to dash to the horse tank first and be prepared to storm the unsuspecting Ernie.

On the designated evening, Dux transported our hot, grimy crew into the barnyard and we bailed out of the old Chevy while the wheels were still spinning. Off we dashed for the horse tank. Ernie had slowly ambled up when suddenly Jack shouted, "Pile him!" Once on the ground, with boys gripping all four of Ernie's jerking feet and hands, Jack proclaimed, "Ernie, you lazy lout, we're throwing you in the hog wallow for goofing off and if you don't hoe your share from now on, you'll get another dose!"

Ernie was terrified and began shouting, "Dux! Uncle Benny, save me!" Strangely, neither of them seemed to hear Ernie's pleas. With

terrible kicking, yanking, shrieking, and dragging we all gave a mighty swing and plopped Ernie into the smelly quagmire. He struggled to his feet with black slime coating his face. He sputtered and spit as he vainly tried to wipe the foul slime from his eyes, nose, and lips. Suddenly, he proclaimed, "It's me. I'm Ernie Herbert Reiger of Oak Street." He must have known the covering of slimy mud made it impossible to recognize him. As he plodded out of the muck, Pop arrived on the scene and remarked, "You're a sight to behold. What's going on with this gang?"

Our vocal leader, Jack, explained the situation. While the rest of us stripped off our clothes for a cool plunge in the horse tank, Ernie had to be hosed down to remove the sludge from his entire body, clothes, and boots before he could take a swim. We were never reprimanded, convincing us Ernie had earned his reward.

When we reached the cactus pasture the following morning, it was amazing to all of us to see Ernie grab the first hoe and begin chopping. Each of us learned a lasting lesson from the hog wallow ordeal. Always carry your full share of the load plus do a little extra.

There is no cure for laziness, but being part of a large family helps.

CHAPTER SIXTEEN

Snakes in the Silo

With our escapades around the ranch, there was always an encounter with some sort of snake. We soon learned that Ernie had a profound obsession for snakes of any size or color. Pop had already cautioned him about rattlesnakes which were abundant in the prairie dog town on the ranch. Consequently, Ernie had confined himself to bull snakes or garter snakes, capturing them anytime one was spotted. All the other cousins avoided the writhing, slippery creatures and were more than glad to "sic" Ernie onto any loose snakes.

One summer afternoon we cousins completed our cactus hoeing early and were looking for some adventure. Someone came up with the idea to go gaze down into the old twenty-foot-deep pit silos. The concrete walls resounded with an echo as we took turns poking our heads into the two foot opening through the red tiled walls, shouting

 loudly, and listening for the echo. The old silo had been used for storing sorghum ensilage in early ranch days but later abandoned due to the intensive hand labor necessary to bring the silage to the ground level for feeding cattle. When Ernie's turn came, he peered into the silo depths and as fate would have

it, he spotted one huge bull snake sunning itself on the silo floor. His "snake-itis" erupted and nothing would do but an attempt to capture the quivering reptile. All the cousins finally agreed that we would cooperate in the effort and concluded that a long lariat rope would be stout enough to lower Ernie down the silo wall to capture the snake. Peter Rabbit, who was the youngest, was directed to go to the horse barn and fetch a strong rope.

We tied an end loop in the lariat for Ernie's foot, and then tied a hand loop higher up. We tested the loop distances on the ground and had Ernie wedge his boot into the lower loop, then tightly grab the hand loop. Jack helped stuff Ernie, ropes attached, through the silo opening. The rest of us were lined up on the ground, grasping the lariat firmly as Ernie disappeared over the sidewall. The rough concrete at the silo opening created considerable drag and made it less strenuous for our crew to slowly lower away. We kept moving closer to the silo opening to lower Ernie into the pit. Just as we were nearly to the end of our rope, a loud yell from Ernie echoed up the silo walls that he was on the silo floor. We were relieved he made it down safely, finally realizing that a fall would probably have been fatal.

Ernie had a way with snakes and in no time flat he had the five-foot bull snake captured and coiling around his arm like a long-lost pet. He was so enthralled that he forgot all about the plan to bring the snake to the surface. Finally, Jack got Ernie's attention by shouting, "I heard Blallen say there was a big rattler in one of those holes in the tile wall near the silo floor." Ernie came to life and shouted he would send the snake up. He put the critter's head through the hand loop and tightened it down firmly, then yelled to hoist away. Halfway up, the bull snake wriggled free and dropped back to the silo floor. Ernie was undaunted as he was so anxious to succeed and encouraged us to hoist the snake upward a second time. Two more attempts resulted in failure.

The Kansas sun was setting and the silo grew darker as dusk approached. Jack shouted to Ernie, "Forget the snake and grab hold of the lariat so we can hoist you out." All went well for the first foot, then Ernie's dead weight on the rope created incredible friction dragging over the rough silo opening. We couldn't budge him another inch. Jack urged us to tug and pull with all our might which we did without success. He finally shouted to Ernie we were letting him down and going for help. The thought of a big rattler had Ernie worried and he yelled to hurry up. Since Jack was a big talker, he was elected to run to the barn to get two hundred and fifty pound Blallen to help with the rescue.

"Cri-min-nent-ly. You ornery kids!" Blallen exclaimed. "Why in the world did you ever let Ernie talk you into such a dumb idea? I got more to do than fiddle around with some snake-happy greenhorn." Jack finally convinced Blallen that we were desperate so he plodded to the silo and took the lead position on the lariat with all of us pulling stoutly behind him. His added strength and heft was enough to offset the drag of Ernie's weight on the concrete wall. With all of us pulling, grunting, and groaning after each tug on the rope, we finally saw Ernie's head peering through the silo opening. He was so relieved to be back safely on the ground and the loss of the bull snake was forgotten.

Blallen let Ernie know in no uncertain terms that if he ever pulled such a dumb stunt again he could just stay down there. We all learned a good lesson from the experience, realizing one should always give some thought to the repercussions of any wild ideas before getting too involved.

You only live once. Think twice.

CHAPTER SEVENTEEN

Tom Proves His Feline Agility

The main source of reference and information in the 1930s was the *Book of Knowledge* encyclopedia. My folks had three sets of large encyclopedias including *Collier's, World Book,* and the *Book of Knowledge.* The latter was our favorite because it contained interesting figures and facts. The twenty volume set consisted of nineteen volumes plus the last volume which was an index for the entire set. It was stored in a shiny, two-shelf mahogany bookcase where we were instructed to always return any volume after we finished using it.

One day Mama was reading to Peter Rabbit Rusco and me the facts regarding the feline families of cats and their great ability to land on their feet when they leapt or fell from some height. Due to their  great sense of balance and agility, they always landed on all fours. Later, we thought more about the interesting facts and decided to conduct an experiment with one of our larger barn cats.

As much as I loved my dogs, I didn't have near as much love for the many half-wild cats that roamed around the barn and outbuildings. Our largest feline was a heavy, strong jet black tomcat with a star on his forehead. Tom always showed up at the cow barn at milking time. He enjoyed having warm milk squirted into his mouth directly from a cow's teat as we were milking her. He would follow the stream of warm milk right up towards the cow to the point of placing his paws on the knee of the milker.

Peter Rabbit and I decided Tom would be a great cat for the big test to see how good he was at landing on his feet. We knew he was a big, strong cat of twelve to fifteen pounds and he was not accustomed to being handled or petted. Pete and I dreamed up a plan to capture Tom so that we could conduct our experiment. Our idea was to have Cousin Ernie do the milking and squirt a steady stream of milk into Tom's mouth until he stood on his hind legs with his paws on Ernie's knee.

At milking time the next morning, Tom was on hand. Ernie was milking and began squirting milk into Tom's open mouth. We positioned ourselves behind Tom and were decked out with a pair of Pop's old work gloves to protect our hands from Tom's sharp claws and teeth. While Tom was enjoying his breakfast, Peter Rabbit and I moved in for the capture. I grabbed his strong, front legs right behind his claws and Peter Rabbit gripped his hind legs. Tom began jerking and lurching to get free but we gripped even tighter and started out of the cow barn down the hill to the ranch house.

Tom was growling and jerking as we stretched him out between us, giving us a hard time while we made our way to the lower south porch of the house. This porch was below ground level but overlooked another lower floor that was also built below ground level

in the canyon. We reached the porch railing, gave a hefty swing, and let Tom go sailing through the air to the courtyard below us. To our amazement and delight, he landed on all four feet, gave a piercing yowl, and dashed for the

canyons and out of sight. We didn't see Tom for several days until he eventually showed up for morning milking, drinking cautiously from the cats' milk pan far away from any human contact.

Since Tom passed our test with flying colors, we thought it would be even better to test his ability from a top porch at the ranch house which was another twelve feet higher. We had to wait more than a week for Tom to come close to the milker as he became bolder and forgot about his flying experience. Eventually, Ernie was able to lure him in with a warm stream of milk. Pete and I captured Tom again. Tom was lurching, howling, hissing, and jerking even more violently this time as we made our way from the barn to the house. He must have known what was coming and it was all we could do to hang on to him.

We made our way to the top porch and gave a mighty swing to send Tom sailing into the courtyard. Due to the higher position and perhaps a heftier launch, Tom went flying all the way to the clothes lines in the courtyard, an obstacle we had forgotten was there. He landed directly on one of the clothes lines, right in the middle of his body, which launched him into the air again as he gave out another blood-curdling screech. Amazingly, he landed on his feet again, let out a yowl, and tore off into the canyons. It was weeks before we saw Tom at the barn.

Peter Rabbit and I were so excited about Tom's amazing flights and landings that we could hardly wait to tell Mama all about it. It thrilled us to know that what we learned from the encyclopedia was true. She was none too pleased with us over the entire experiment and strongly instructed us to never throw any more cats from the porch.

Children need to be taught,
but they also must be allowed to teach themselves.

CHAPTER EIGHTEEN

Dux and the Knock-out Drops

Something exciting or unusual seemed to occur daily at the ranch due to the numbers and diversity of people who were living, working or visiting there. It seemed that the cousins had more than their share of pranks, wild episodes, and near catastrophes.

Dux and fuzzy-headed Billy, a.k.a. Woolo, bunked together in the boy's room on a lower floor of the four-story ranch house, which in bygone days had housed muleskinners and cowboys. Woolo had a compulsion for science and especially chemistry experiments. He thrived on mixing up strange concoctions from the science kit Mama had given him and from supplies borrowed from the ranch storeroom which we referred to as the store.

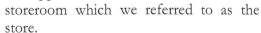

The store was a large room on the south wing of the ranch house. It served as a general store from the early 1900s, when there were twenty to twenty-five hired hands and cowboys to feed, five tenant families, the Marriage family, and a constant stream of visitors. The storeroom housed cases of canned goods, dried foods, vinegar, and baking supplies that included forty-eight pound sacks of Kelley's

Famous Flour and twenty pound sacks of sugar. Smaller tin cans of Clabbergirl Baking Powder, Arm & Hammer Baking Soda, Carey Salt, black pepper, and a conglomerate of interesting looking boxes, bottles, and cartons also lined the shelves. These provisions offered an unlimited supply of ingredients for Woolo's experiments.

We cousins were intrigued watching his mixing techniques, which produced much fizzing and foaming as he added more ingredients. Sometimes his concoctions created a mild eruption which fascinated all of us. Why nothing ever exploded, we never knew. Thank goodness there was no gunpowder left on the shelves in the

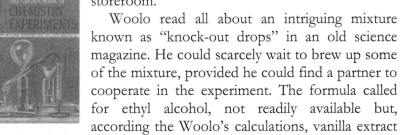

storeroom. Woolo read all about an intriguing mixture known as "knock-out drops" in an old science magazine. He could scarcely wait to brew up some of the mixture, provided he could find a partner to cooperate in the experiment. The formula called for ethyl alcohol, not readily available but, according the Woolo's calculations, vanilla extract would be a good substitute. He convinced Dux to participate in the knock-out drops experiment. But, Woolo cautioned Dux, "You must follow the directions to the letter to avoid any toxic reactions."

The night for the big experiment finally arrived. Our gang gathered in the boy's room with Dux and Woolo who told him, "I'm going to prop you up in bed in a good position to better participate in this interesting experiment. I've put a clock, paper, and pencil here handy to record your reactions as they occur." We cousins were intrigued by the detailed preparations and the solemn, serious demeanor displayed by Woolo.

Woolo carefully administered the proper dosage of knock-out drops, handed Dux a magazine and told him, "I want you to read aloud to test the effectiveness of the drops." Dux began to read. Five minutes later he began reading more slowly, followed by slurred speech. Then total silence as he dropped the magazine and passed out. Woolo was elated that all was going as the experiment directions had described. He watched the clock tick off fifteen long minutes. All of us were silent, including Dux, as we watched the motionless subject of Woolo's experiment.

Woolo consulted the instructions in the science magazine again to be sure about what should happen next since Dux showed no signs of arousing. The subject should have awakened after twelve to fifteen minutes. By this time, Woolo was getting concerned and nervous but he decided to wait five more minutes and observe Dux. The Big Ben alarm clock by the bed seemed to tick even louder in the dead silence. The time was up and Woolo was really becoming frantic. He began shaking Dux and calling out, "Dux, Dux, can you hear me?"

He was pounding him and making every effort to awaken him. Fear set in. Woolo began shouting, "Dux, speak to me!" but to no avail. Woolo panicked. He dashed up the stairs to the third floor where our family lived screaming, "Help, help!"

Vivian was home and quickly followed Woolo down the stairs as he breathlessly explained the predicament. When she got to Dux's bedside he was still out cold and Woolo kept shouting, "Dux, speak to me!" She draped a very cold, wet cloth over his head, hoping the shock might spark some reaction, but there was none. We were skeptical that it was all just pretend and a big joke on Dux's part, but we weren't certain.

Finally in a very loud voice, Vivian commanded, "Dux, if you don't quit acting and wake up, I'm going to call Dr. McLaughlin in Greensburg to drive clear out here. That will cost a lot and you'll be in big, big trouble."

Apparently the cold cloth or the threatening words or both, penetrated Dux's skull, and he began a low, guttural, groaning sound followed by flopping his arms and legs. How relieved all of us were that he wasn't paralyzed by the drops. Again Woolo shouted over and over, "Dux speak to me!" After what seemed an eternity, Dux began mumbling and eventually his words were understandable.

He opened his eyes and exclaimed, "Vivian, what are you doing down here?"

"Trying to figure out what you two dummies have been doing," she exclaimed. Thirty minutes later, Dux seemed to be near normal except for what he reported as a supposed bad headache and feeling very tired. Vivian decided he was out of danger, but admonished them, "This case is not closed unless you both promise never again to experiment with knock-out drugs!" We never knew if the knock-out drops actually worked or was Dux just a superb actor?

That summer of fun and wild experiences eventually ended as the cousins returned home for the start of the next school year. We said heartfelt good-byes with the aspirations of a city cousins' reunion at the ranch the next summer. As the last of the cousins drove up the lane from the ranch, Blallen was relieved that the boys were out of his hair as he muttered, "Happy day. Happy day." Although Blallen appeared gruff when the city cousins were around, it was evident to me that he actually enjoyed the extra activity and excitement, and like me, he missed them as everything reverted back to normal after they returned home.

It's amazing how much trouble you can get into
when you don't have anything else to do.

CHAPTER NINETEEN

School Days in the Dirty Thirties

By the time I was old enough to go to school, most of the one room schools around Kiowa County had been closed. It had become too costly to keep the schools open and the rural population was dropping as fast as the price of wheat and cattle. Even our beautiful brick school house on the ranch had been closed. It was an impressive structure with large windows, a bell tower, and wide concrete steps that led to the front door. It had a large classroom, study room, and a full basement. It even had electricity supplied from the ranch house Delco system. It was a sad day for my parents when they decided it was time to close Sunflower School and send everyone to town school.

It was during these mid-thirties that I reached the momentous age of six and was permitted to begin the first grade. I was the pig-tail in the Weaver family of five. Marjorie was a junior in college, Vivian was a junior in high school, Doris was a freshman, and Kenny was in fifth grade. His tales of school pals and fun times during recess made me even more anxious to begin school. Although I was a bit bashful and shy with only older siblings as playmates, I was eager to ride the bus to town school and have friends of my own age.

The Mullinville town school had two separate one-room, white frame buildings housing the first and second grade students,

respectively. The schools had been moved to town when they were no longer needed for rural students. Each building had a small cloak room for hanging coats and a place for storing overshoes in muddy or snowy weather. The shelf above each coat hook was for lunch boxes, ranging from rectangular tin boxes to round half-gallon or gallon pails, which had formerly been filled with corn syrup, molasses, or honey.

The most common sandwiches were hard fried egg, peanut butter and jelly, or fried cured ham. Some were made with homemade bread and others with store-bought white bread. Our food was wrapped in waxed paper, but it didn't take long for it to get dry. We often traded sandwiches as we grew tired of our own "brand" from home. I looked forward to trading my pint jar of Kool-aid mixed with sand hill plum juice to Weenie Rudd for a banana or a Hydrox cookie.

Our favorite recess activities were the merry-go-round, swings, giant strides swing, and the slide. Sometimes we played Run-Sheep-Run or Drop the Handkerchief, a favorite of the girls.

I was introduced to a smelly, two-hole outhouse in the first grade. It was quite a shock to me and my siblings before me since we had grown up with running water and an indoor flush toilet at the ranch. Both the first and second grade buildings had separate outhouses which took some getting used to not only because of the aroma but also the trauma of going to the outhouse on cold winter days. The draft from the strong Kansas winds took care of the aroma but chilled us while we "did our business." We really felt like graduates when we reached third grade and moved to the big brick grade school building which had inside toilets.

Miss Gertrude Likes taught first grade at Mullinville for nearly forty years. In fact, almost every Mullinville area resident under forty-five years of age had her as their first teacher. She was a tall, stately maiden lady with jet black hair pulled back in a bun behind her head.

Although patient and kindly, she believed in keeping order in our classroom of twenty-two first graders who started school in 1933. All country kids rode the school bus and the few town kids walked to school.

Eldon Weaver, Eulalio Espinosa, Glenn Headrick, Dorl Rader, Eugene Rudd

Eulalio Espinosa, a jovial and cheerful Mexican boy, Glenn Headrick, and I were often afflicted by laughing and giggling fits during recess. We tended to carry that commotion back to class, much to Miss Likes' dismay. We weren't disruptive enough to deserve a paddling. But each of us at one time or another were told to crawl under the teacher's old oak desk where we were banished to isolation in the dark knee-space of her desk. That embarrassment tended to sober us up rather quickly.

An amusing episode happened on one occasion when I was serving my time under her desk. As Miss Likes finished reading recitation, she apparently had forgotten about my location. She sat down at her desk and as her feet engaged a body, she nearly leaped out of her chair. The whole class giggled and I came close to a paddling. We often thought she must have imagined a stray dog had wandered in for a nap under her desk.

Miss Likes was strong on grammar and the use of correct English. Many kids in those days used the word "ain't" and that word was on her elimination list. She drew what looked like jail bars around the word ain't on the blackboard. If ain't ever escaped from some kid's mouth, down came a big black rag, suspended from a cup hook near the jail drawing on the blackboard. Miss Likes proceeded to tie the black rag over the mouth of the culprit. Believe me, one time with the black rag was enough to cure the most perpetual abuser. Her method apparently was highly effective as I have no recollection of hearing ain't spoken in the second grade.

Miss Likes loved books and wanted each child to become a good reader. A book of her choice was sent home with every student on

Friday afternoon. Each of us were to read the book over the weekend and bring it back Monday morning with a verification slip, signed by our folks, stating that their child had read the book. She treated library books as if they were precious commodities and wrapped each one in a sheet of newspaper and tied it with used butcher string to protect it on the trip home from school. Upon its return, the book was to be re-wrapped as before to protect it from weather and soiling. Monday morning a shiny stick-on gold star was placed beside each child's name for every book read.

Miss Margaret Keeler taught second grade for thirty-eight years. She, too, was a maiden lady but more stern than Miss Likes. Her dark brown, piercing eyes could instill fear into any wayward second grader. Eulalio, Glenn and I were still good pals in second grade and would be laughing and giggling upon returning to class from recess. Miss Keeler expected us to shut off all that giggling and labeled us her "giggle-boxes." Sometimes we slipped up and disrupted class, resulting in each of us being placed in a different corner of the one room building with our noses high in the air. Her sternness and the embarrassment toned us down promptly and we could eventually return to our respective desks.

Uncle Wiggily Longears was Miss Keeler's favorite fictional character. He was a large, elderly rabbit who walked with a crutch. Stories from the Uncle Wiggily series were published one day each week in the *Hutchinson News*. Miss Keeler had clipped each episode for years and pasted those newsprint stories in a huge scrapbook. The pages were yellowed with age but each day after recess, she would read us one exciting episode to get us settled down for spelling class.

Miss Keeler would let Eulalio write the alphabet on the blackboard as our penmanship example. I always admired Eulalio, not only for his intelligence, but also for his beautiful, cursive writing. He could form the alphabet letters, both lower case and capitals, exactly like the penmanship charts.

Third grade was highly anticipated—we thought we had reached the big time to graduate to the large, two story grade school housing third through eighth graders. Old Mr. Harrison, the school custodian, was a slight, slender man who was always friendly to new arrivals. It was exciting to watch him heave-ho the heavy rope and ring the giant cast iron school bell mounted on the two story building. The loud clanging of that bell beckoned us back to class after recess. We boys were usually in a big game of "shinny" and it was disappointing to have to stop the action to get back to studying. Shinny was played much like soccer—the ball could only be kicked without the use of hands. Often a wild kick that missed the ball produced skinned shins for the closest opponent, hence the name, shinny.

Miss Hentz was our third grade teacher. She was a kindly, motherly-type maiden lady, liked by all students. She did keep order but in a more compassionate disciplinary style. She gave us a good basis for math facts and by fifth grade we were ciphering on the blackboard.

Miss Wilson, our fifth grade teacher, conducted the ciphering matches which was a procedure involving the entire class. We all went to the blackboards and would write down the problem as she read to us. It might be addition, subtraction, multiplication or division. Miss Wilson read the problem rapidly as we each wrote it on the board. We were to solve it as quickly as possible, then whirl around facing inward.  The last student to turn around took their seat. Then another problem was solved with the same procedure being followed until only two contestants were left standing. Eulalio was quick in math and he and I often ended up ciphering each other until one of us was declared the winner by finishing first on three consecutive problems.

Being the son of the school board president, I was fortunate to attend the annual Mullinville teacher's party and reunion hosted each August at Eagle Canyon Ranch. It was held in honor of all elementary and high school teachers and their spouses. The afternoon and evening event included horseback riding, climbing canyons, games, and wagon rides pulled by Kate and Don, the last mule team left on the ranch after tractors replaced farm equipment pulled by mules.

Blallen was thrilled to be able to serve his homemade donuts, wearing his flour sack apron, as the teachers arrived for the festivities. Mama had taught him how to make cake donuts, fried in hot lard, and sugared by shaking them in a brown paper bag while still warm. The donuts were served on platters along with a choice of hot coffee or apple cider as the guests arrived. Hearing the teachers brag on his donuts did much for Blallen's self-esteem. He loved feeling appreciated and being able to provide his special contribution to the pleasures of the day.

Each year for the reunion Mama chose a different theme as a way to add more fun and creativity to the event. One year each teacher was to come dressed as a funny paper or comic strip character while another year the theme was about Indians with everyone wearing a headband, feather, and colorful Indian blanket. Following a bountiful meal of beef, pork, and chicken with all the trimmings, a talent show with skits, poems,  readings, and recitations ensued. The show was held in the large parlor in the ranch house. Each teacher was to present some act, poem, story, or tale to the other guests gathered at the event. Pop Weaver always recited *Nebuchadnezzar*, a popular poem of that era. It told the tale of a southern sharecropper and his cantankerous mule plowing a cotton field. Mama would often recite *Towser Must Be Tied Tonight* about two young lovers and her father's guard dog that chased the would-be Romeo. Blallen could never be coaxed into performing but he relished the skits, acts, and talent presented.

Uncannily and unbelievably, the only rain ever received in August over the years would invariably happen during the teacher's reunion. The rain would turn the quarter-mile hill from the ranch house to the main driveway into a slippery, clay-covered hill, saturated by the run-off from the higher elevation. It presented quite a challenge to the drivers who had parked in front of the house. Smooth, tread-bare tires on vehicles were common, providing little traction in the mud on the hill. As guests went to their cars to leave, one by one, with wheels spinning, each car was pushed to the top of the hill by three or four men who volunteered to be "pushers." Pop Weaver and Mr. Ezra Fast, a sixth grade teacher, were shoving hard on a '34 Chevy when it suddenly lurched ahead just as Mr. Fast gave a powerful lunge forward. He landed with a splatter, face down in the muddy clay. When he finally got to his feet, he shook his muddy fist and shouted, "What fool would build a house at the bottom of a thirty foot hill?" Pop nearly split laughing at his exclamation. Pop and Blallen were the ones to push the last car up the hill to the flat road leading from the ranch property to the paved road,

concluding another delightful event at Eagle Canyon Ranch.

By sixth grade we felt mighty important when we graduated to the second floor of the grade school building. That was the year we were exposed to the threat of paddlings reserved for unruly boys. The most common causes for a paddling were bad language and fighting during recess. They were administered by Mr. Forrest Cate, a small beady-eyed principal who ruled by fear. We shook in our boots when he would suddenly appear around the corner of the school building during recess. A wide wooden paddle and heavy leather strap were his favorite instruments for thrashings. Deanie Kirk, a skinny, hard-up town kid, was raised in a criminally inclined family which contributed to his delinquency. Deanie was our first exposure to the pornographic drawings and filthy printed materials which he brought to school from home. Mr. Cate had a way of discovering such acts and would take Deanie into his office and lambast him. The office door was purposefully left open to permit Deanie's shrieks and the

splat of the paddle to resound down the entire hallway. Anyone even thinking of mischievous acts quickly lost the urge.

I tried hard to avoid a paddling, not only to dodge the pain of punishment, but to avoid additional trouble and embarrassment to my parents when I went home. And I knew about the only paddling Kenny ever received at school or at least the only one we ever heard about. It was administered by kindly Miss Hentz, the third grade teacher. Kenny sat directly in front of Harlan Cope in a row of old-style wooden school desks. Each desk had an inkwell and a fold-up seat rest. He and Harlan were cutting up when suddenly, Harlan decided to give Kenny a rise by shoving the sharp point of a compass leg up through the fold-up seat slot. Harlan jabbed Kenny in the rear and the resulting shriek and expletive from Kenny earned him a paddling.

The most important things a child can inherit
are fond memories.

CHAPTER TWENTY

Runaway Mules

Eulalio was a smiley-faced Mexican boy in my third grade class at school and one of my favorite pals. There were two large Mexican families in Mullinville, the Rivas and the Espinosas, who lived in old box cars on the Rock Island railroad right-of-way. The box cars were furnished like a house on wheels for the families. The men worked long days as section hands on the track doing tough manual labor.

Eulalio was right smart and I envied his beautiful cursive writing. He could write just like the penmanship charts and his writing even put our teacher to shame. My father always stressed neat penmanship and Pop had a beautiful, artistic writing style of his own. So, I probably noticed Eulalio's handwriting ability even more. We had ciphering matches in arithmetic at school in which Eulalio and I usually ended up trying to outdo each other by adding or dividing the fastest.

Eulalio was a hard worker like his father and delivered The *Hutchinson News* all over Mullinville. He walked his route every day for over a year to save enough money to buy a flashy bicycle with balloon tires, horn,

speedometer, headlight, and taillight. None of us kids from the farm had a bicycle and we really made over Eulalio's shiny blue bike with the chrome trim.

Jesus Espinosa, Eulalio's father, wouldn't let him ride his new bike to school for fear it would get banged up or worn out by kids who wanted to ride it, especially those of us who weren't very good riders anyway. My only hope to get to ride Eulalio's bike was to invite him to ride his bike out to the ranch so we could ride horses. I knew he would love to ride my horse while I rode his bike. That scheme was a dandy and we had many good times  sharing our different modes of transportation.

One fall Saturday while Eulalio was out to play with me for the day, Pop needed help to drive a team of mules, Kate and Don, back to the ranch from a distant sumac cane field while pulling a hay rack load of bundled feed. Pop loaded the wagon, making sure he had a full load, but not so heavy that Kate would throw her usual fit. If the load was getting too heavy and the ground was soft, Kate would start to paw the dirt. When a few more bundles were added and it became too much for her, she would throw her front leg over the neck yoke which brought everything to a halt. The only way to get her leg loose was to unfasten the harness, drop the neck yoke to free up her leg, then put the harness on again. That crafty old mule taught us it was less trouble to let her have a lighter load than to overload the wagon.

Pop made us a good seat of four feed bundles crosswise on top of the high load of feed. Then Pop gave us instructions about paying attention to business, holding tight to the reins, and no trotting. He instructed, "You boys will have a dandy seat here on these feed bundles. Here are the reins. Remember, old Kate and Don can get spooked pretty easily so mind your business and keep them in a walk."

After about an hour of driving the team back to the ranch, we were getting bored and like boys will do, and we started wrestling around in the feed. Sure enough, we dropped the reins. I wasn't too worried since I knew that horses and mules can find their way home on a familiar road. When the end of the rein slapped Don on the rump, he started to trot, taking Kate with him. Eulalio and I panicked when we realized we had picked up speed and began to imagine an upset hay wagon with us underneath the load. By now the mules were close to home and trotting even faster, so the ride was getting even rougher. Fearing the worst, we each grabbed a big bundle of feed to break our fall and bailed out. As luck would have it, the mules were true creatures of habit, unlike certain boys, and stayed between the roadside ditches until they arrived with the load at the cattle guard nearest the home barn lot.

Pop was way ahead of us in the Chevy and led the mules on into the barn. He probably thought we were a sight to behold as he saw us trudging down the dusty lane a half-mile away, but he knew we weren't hurt. Letting us walk the rest of the way back was a step-by-step reminder about heeding good advice when boys are sent to do a man's job.

In school, you're taught a lesson and then given a test.
In life, you're given a test that teaches you a lesson.

CHAPTER TWENTY-ONE

Neighbor Visitations in the 1930s

Periodically, Pop would decide it was time to visit neighbors whose land adjoined Eagle Canyon Ranch. When the weather was bad, if the ground was wet, or when there were only a few unfinished ranch duties seemed to be the best times for his visits. Pop had a concern for people due to his upbringing as the son of a Methodist preacher and because of his civic duty as an elected representative to the Kansas Legislature. I was always thrilled when Pop would let me accompany him, riding on my favorite bay pony, Toots, and Pop on his stalwart strawberry roan mare, Old Roan or on Buck. This was one of the few leisure activities we enjoyed together as father and

son. It was easier to travel by horseback through the canyons to the neighbors' houses than to crank up the old '29 Chevy and take a roundabout route on the county roads and farm lanes.

The John Dean family lived two miles southeast of the ranch. They were from Tennessee, settling south of Mullinville in the mid-twenties. John left a widow and two bachelor sons, Henley and Pryor. The boys were her only companions, making her quite lonely, and it cheered her to have any visitors. I was intrigued by the Tennessee colloquial lingo spoken by the Deans. "Haint" was a frequently used term and "I hain't got none" was a common expression.

Mrs. Dean baked homemade sourdough bread using starter dough in place of yeast. The strong flavored bread was a real treat for Pop,  although I never understood why. After a few minutes of friendly chatter, Pop would remark, "Mrs. Dean, little Eldon has never tasted your delicious sourdough bread." This remark prompted her to head for the kitchen and whack off two healthy slices of bread lathered by a generous coating of homemade butter.

 I nearly choked on my first bite, not only because of the strong sour taste, but also from the bitter whang of the butter. I learned later that butter left sitting out of the icebox for a few days became very rancid and strong in flavor. Pop had insisted to us at an early age that we should not waste food. He told us there were starving children in the world who would welcome a bread crust, so I was obligated to eat the whole slice. I begged Pop to refrain from asking for sourdough bread on future visits.

Son Pryor was a rather paunchy fellow with strong, weathered suspenders and often with a big, black cigar hanging out of his mouth. I was spellbound by his preparation for lighting and smoking a cigar. First, he whacked off one end of the cigar with a pocket knife, then lolled the cigar around in his mouth to moisten it, and finally slobbered all over the cigar before lighting up. Even at my age, I had been taught it was not polite to spit, drool, or slobber and I had never seen an adult with such a habit as Pryor. That was a real eye opener for a naïve nine-year-old.

Oldest son, Henley, was known as a "boozer" and addicted to

alcohol which further added to his mother's woes. And Henley preferred tailor-made cigarettes, not cigars. He always had bloodshot eyes and shaky hands. Like clockwork, every Saturday night Henley would jump in their old Essex and head for Bucklin to locate the local bootlegger who always had powerful whiskey for a price. Kansas was "dry" in those days, so there was not a bar or speak-easy or liquor store where alcohol was sold. Henley would consume a fifth of whiskey straight from the bottle before midnight, then attempt to drive back to the farm, weaving back and forth between the country road ditches. Fortunately, normal people were home in bed at that time which protected them from his hazardous, wild driving.

Every Monday morning, a long-necked whiskey bottle would lie in the ditch along the road running through Eagle Canyon Ranch. The only good derived from Henley's weekly escapade was the fact that a long-necked bottle was ideal for drenching equines. Occasionally, one faithful mule, Don, would develop the colic. Don and Kate were a mule team used on the ranch so Don was too valuable to be sick for any length of time and not able to work. When Don would begin to roll, lie down and get up, or kick at his belly, we knew it was time for a treatment. Pop would fill the discarded empty whiskey bottle with warm linseed oil and ram it back into Don's throat, causing him to glug down the whole contents of the bottle. The thick, lubricating tonic did the trick and cured his colic.

When we prepared to leave Dean's place, the boys would accompany us back to our horses tied to their yard fence. Pop would stop and take Henley aside to talk about his drinking problem. I can vividly remember their conversation. "Friend Henley," Pop would remark. "You are such a fine neighbor and good friend. It grieves me to see you becoming a slave to that demon alcohol. Your must get a hold on yourself and break this habit before it kills you." Pop had heard many sermons from his father's pulpit about the ill effects of a drinking habit.

Henley's stock reply was, "B. O., (my dad's initials) you are probably right. I have tried many times to quit drinking but about Friday afternoon or Saturday morning I begin getting the shakes and an awful craving for a drink, so bad that by Saturday I just have to head for Bucklin to buy a bottle." Unfortunately, Pop was never able to convince Henley to stop his heavy drinking and Henley died in his early fifties of cirrhosis of the liver.

The Horsehead Ranch, operated by Weldon and Nellie Douglass, adjoined the Dean's on the south and was usually our next stop. They were fortunate to have a spring-fed creek running through their valley, providing plenty of moisture in a rich, sandy loam soil ideal for  watermelon production. It was no secret that Pop was a watermelon fan and Weldon always offered him as many as he wanted. Pop once described a watermelon feed as "the deepest pleasure of the American boy. Watch a group of boys eating a half of a ripe watermelon and each will be wearing a smile from ear to ear." Weldon's patch was once raided by Eagle Canyon Ranch hands on a moonlit fall night. Two of their daughters, Marion and Virginia, were around the same age as my sisters and came to the ranch to play. Mama and Nellie were great friends although they rarely had much time to spend together.

The next neighbor south of Douglass' was Louie Loveland, a short, beady-eyed Southerner who tried to raise enough crops on his hilly, hard clay farm to feed his large family. His extremely thin, hardworking wife, Vera, was bedraggled by a raft of kids and little food. Pop felt sorry for the entire family and remembered times as a child when he and his ten siblings barely had enough to eat. Pop would periodically station himself in Sager's grocery store in Mullinville, asking patrons to donate a few grocery items to a large box for the Loveland family. Louie tended to let his pride overcome  good judgment and wanted no one to think he was taking handouts. In those days, men took enormous pride in taking care of their family responsibilities and it was a humiliating stigma of failure to accept food, money, or clothing from others. Consequently, Pop would manage to unload the grocery box at Loveland's kitchen door where Vera gratefully accepted the food with tears in her eyes. Seeing a mother's humble tears was another sobering impression for me as a nine-year-old.

The next farm south of Loveland's was the Canfields, where Mrs. Canfield and her unusual son, Harvey, lived. Harvey was a lean, lanky, pointed-faced fellow, who when goaded and guided by his mother, managed to get crops planted and harvested. Mrs. Canfield was rather poorly with a health condition she had endured for many years. It restricted her mobility thus making any visitors all the more welcome. After Old Slinky had been done in by the Collett boys, we were careful not to mention the absence of that mean old dog. With him out of the way, we were much less apprehensive about stopping to visit them.

Occasionally, we visited the Bill Collett family southeast of Canfield's. The Colletts were from the deep South and very softly pronounced their "r's." An example of this occurred when we found a dead Marriage Mulley cow in the Eagle Lake pasture, not far from Collett's. Her death was mysterious; however, Bill diagnosed her demise as having been poisoned by the "laakspuh" or what we called larkspur weed. One son, Ed, was quite enterprising and wanted to earn some money during those hard times. He took up breaking horses to the saddle for fifteen dollars per head. This included feeding and care during the month of breaking.

The Colletts had been hearing strange sounds and thumping noises at night under the floor of their bedroom. After repeated

pleadings from Mrs. Collett, Bill finally crawled under the house and found a litter of baby skunks. Enterprising Ed once read they made excellent house pets. He collected the babies in a sturdy cardboard box and then hauled them to Bucklin to have the local veterinarian remove their scent glands. He had no trouble selling them to friends and neighbors which gave him some "jingle in his jeans."

Bill and Ma White lived two miles east of Colletts and too close for comfort due to their criminally inclined nature. They were from the back hills of Tennessee and were suspected of operating a moonshine still while there. Their two sons, Clem and Sam, were in and out of jail so frequently it was nearly impossible to keep track of them. They were avoided by neighbors as much possible. Near neighbors would notice that a steer mysteriously disappeared from time to time with no explanation for his absence. The Whites were high on the suspect list.

Bill was a puffy-faced, paunchy man sporting a scroungy beard and bloodshot eyes from consuming too much whiskey. Ma was close behind in her looks with greasy, mangy hair, a leather complexion, and snaggle-toothed. Bill Collett reported that when Pa White would come home from the bootlegger half-drunk, Ma would tie his hands to the end gate of their feed wagon, cluck the team into a trot, and trot or half-drag Bill around their barnyard until he sobered up.

Drifters were common during the Depression as men were desperate for work during those trying times. When a drifter wandered onto the White's farm, Ma would cordially invite him to stay by offering board, room, and thirty dollars a month for his farm labor. Bill was a lazy lout and both sons spent more time in prison than on the farm so very little farming was accomplished.

Two different neighbors reported what they knew of the White's cash-free farm labor scheme. A drifter could be found on the main road, thumbing a ride, then relating his fearful plight. When payday came, after a month of long, hot hours in the field, Ma would call the drifter into the kitchen where she kept a double-barreled shotgun. She would lay the shotgun across her greasy jeans, look the unfortunate laborer in the eye and proclaim, "Thar's seven men buried in yon corral and there'll be anotheren afore night 'lessen you hightail it offen our farm!" Mr. Collett once picked up such a hitchhiker who was anxious to put many, many miles between him and Ma White.

Pop's visits to the White's were prompted by various incidents but not social calls. One such situation involved Mr. Moorhead, a Texas rancher. Cash money was mighty scarce and various avenues were attempted to obtain some extra income. If spring rains happened to green up the buffalo grass pastures, Pop would take in steers by the month to fatten on the grass in Eagle Lake pasture. Mr. Moorhead would ship in lean, hungry steers to Kansas hoping to put some pounds on their rangy carcasses.

In late fall, Mr. Moorhead would come to settle up and pick up his much heavier critters. After the roundup, the count was one steer short. We found none dead in our pasture indicating he might have drifted into some neighboring pasture. The Whites were the first suspects due to such a shady history as suspected cattle rustlers. With this in mind, Pop and Mr. Moorhead drove to the White's farm in hopes of finding the missing steer, possibly confined in their corral or barn. Bill was moseying around the yard when Pop and Mr.

Moorhead arrived. They exchanged polite howdy-dos, then stated their mission. Bill, of course, denied any extra steers were on their premises. Mr. Moorhead then asked if they could look around in the barn. Just as they reached the barn door, the bellow of a steer caught their attention. Lo and behold, there was old Brindle, the only steer Mr. Moorhead owned with that coloration. Upon closer examination, a big Flying M brand was noticed on his left hip. That ended the discussion and soon Brindle was loaded in the stock trailer headed for the ranch.

The Sprout ranch lay two miles east of White's. Scott and Marilyn Sprout and their widower son, Clarence, operated their spread. Marilyn was raising their two granddaughters. A unique sight for me on their ranch was an aged cottonwood tree with such a massive trunk it took extended arms of ten men to encircle it.

The Sprouts were unusually tall people, with Scott at six feet four inches, and Marilyn close behind at six feet tall. Her unusual feat was the ability to kick her foot higher than her head, often touching the casing over a doorway. One Sunday afternoon the Sprouts came to the ranch for a visit. Someone mentioned Marilyn's high kicking ability and she always seemed open to giving a demonstration. She walked up to the open parlor doorway and aligned herself under the upper casing. She gave an extremely high kick such that the effort jerked her supporting foot off the floor. She landed on her back on the hardwood floor. The men rushed to give her aid and, amazingly, she was not injured but quite shaken up. That was one high kick I will never forget.

Papa and Mamma Thach had land adjoining Eagle Canyon Ranch farmland on the north and pastureland on the east. Papa Thach was a small, quiet man unlike Mamma who did most of the talking. Her favorite pastime was listening in on the party line to neighbors' private telephone conversations. This weakened the telephone signal thus making it awfully difficult to hear the other person on the call. Long distance calls were rare due to the expense. My three sisters, Marjorie, Vivian, and Doris, were away at college and were advised to only make a long distance call home for an emergency or dire need. Such an occasion came up for Vivian. The old oak wall phone rang three long rings and a short. Each household on the line could hear the telephone ring, but this was our signal that the call was for us. Pop answered and was straining to hear Vivian, likewise for her.

Finally, she blurted out, "If Mrs. Thach would just hang up we would probably be able to hear each other." A sudden click on the line let them know that Vivian's remark did the trick.

Papa Thach apparently craved recognition. Each fall when new car license plates were to be on sale at the courthouse in Greensburg, Papa would drive to the courthouse at five o'clock in the morning and sit by the door in order to get the first plate issued in Kiowa County, 85-1, Kansas. The one hundred and five counties in Kansas were numbered by population starting with Kansas City located in Wyandotte, Wichita in Sedgwick, and Topeka in Shawnee being the top three. Kiowa County was well down the list in population at number eighty-five.

The three Thach children, Ray, Wayne, and Ruth, were all adopted although each from different families. Papa apparently had a mean streak because periodically he would give Ray a sound thrashing with a bridle rein. During the ordeal, if the wind was right, we could hear Ray yelling from a mile and a half across the pasture to the ranch house. In those days, child abuse was never mentioned and no one meddled directly with the personal affairs of a neighbor. However, if the offense was too great, the parents might be anonymously reported to the adoption agency. Ray was a husky kid and soon more than equaled Papa in size and stature, putting an end to the thrashings.

The Thach dog, Rags, was a scroungy Airedale that chased every car making a turn at the Thach corner. Rags chased, barked, growled, and chewed at the tires of each vehicle passing by their place. He had been run over repeatedly and was evidently a slow learner. Such mishaps had misaligned his mangy carcass to the point he ran at about a forty-five degree angle. We always laughed at his gait and Pop often remarked, "That mangy dog isn't worth shooting." Rags was an odd sight.

Papa Thach applied for the County Varmint Control officer job. He was the person designated to be contacted for eradication of  pests. Prairie dogs were quite prevalent on Eagle Canyon Ranch, digging holes, burrowing, building mounds, and killing out the buffalo grass around their mounds or towns. In addition, it was dangerous to ride horses through a prairie dog town for fear the horse would step in a hole and break a leg, not to mention the rattlesnakes they attracted. The courthouse referred us to Papa for assistance in eradication of the pesky varmints. Papa would arrive with a gallon can of a mixture he called Hokey Pokey, a pair of tongs, and cotton balls. He would grab a cotton ball with his tongs, dip it in the deadly liquid, and drop one in each prairie dog hole. We threw a chunk of cardboard over the opening, then promptly covered it with two shovels full of dirt. As the strong liquid evaporated, the deadly gas asphyxiated  the prairie dogs. However, my father could hardly bear to kill off the entire population, so usually one hole was left untreated and gradually the prairie dog population would make a recovery.

The McCaslins, from the old country, lived east of the Thach place. Pop and I would sometimes pay them a visit. They had no children and welcomed visitors. The McCaslins both spoke with a 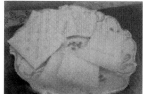 strong Irish brogue which was most intriguing to a nine-year-old.

After several minutes of visiting, Pop would tactfully remark, "Mrs. McCaslin, little Eldon just loves your mighty fine yellow cheese." She had learned the art of cheesemaking in Ireland from her grandmother. His request prompted Mrs. McCaslin to ask Mac to go down into the cellar and find a ripe ball of cheese. Upon his return, she would lay the round block of cheese on a cutting board and whack off the paraffin covering. Then she sliced off some good chunks and served it with soda crackers. What a delicious treat! Pop profusely bragged on the delicious, mellow cheese, no doubt hoping for more on a future visit.

Returning from McCaslin's, we would stop at the Charlie and Charlene Burrton farm, three-fourths of a mile north of Thach's. Their three children, Roger, Euell, and Tibby, were good friends of my sisters. Mrs. Burrton was an exceptional cook and always applauded by the neighbors who ate her meals while on the traveling threshing machine crew as it moved from farm to farm. Their chicken ran free-range, living on spilled grain and grasshoppers, and became delicious fried chicken.

Neighbor Visitations in the 1930s

The John Coolidge family lived three miles east and were a well-educated English family. Mama knew them growing up and always admired them. Mrs. Coolidge was an excellent musician and was Marjorie's first piano teacher. A one-room schoolhouse, Highland School, was located across the road where they promoted cultural evening events such as lyceums and Chautauquas. Pop Weaver often presented his *Nebuchadnezzar* act at their schoolhouse events. Years earlier, they competed in spelling bees, debates, and other events with Sunflower School located on Eagle Canyon Ranch.

The Lutz brothers, Charlie and Alfred, were from Arkansas. Their farm adjoined the northwest corner of the ranch. They were extremely protective of their registered Hereford cowherd and became very disturbed when a two thousand pound Marriage Mulley bull broke into their pasture to mingle and fraternize with their purebred cows. In an attempt to smooth over neighborly relations, Pop would visit the Lutz brothers. One visit near noon, Charlie decided to bake his famous baking powder biscuits to go along with bacon and eggs. He invited Pop to stay for dinner and naturally he accepted. Charlie baked in a stovepipe oven above a Topsy wood stove, much like the Topsy stove my folks used when they first set up housekeeping in 1913. The boys had fresh honey and home churned butter. Pop was so hungry he overate and became quite ill when he arrived back home two hours later. He did, however, blame it on too much honey and biscuits and not Charlie's cooking skills.

All these visits with our many memorable neighbors gave me a broader perspective of the differences in backgrounds and families, plus a much greater appreciation of my parents' strong moral values and Christian beliefs. Those friendly visitations tended to create better understandings and improve relationships between neighbors in the community.

A good neighbor will have good neighbors.

CHAPTER TWENTY-TWO

Shopping in the City – Dodge City

When Blallen heard the Weaver girls were coming home from college for the summer, he would exhibit a rare glimmer of optimism by exclaiming, "Happy day!" which was his favorite response when cheered by some happening or situation. He seemed to have a special place in his heart for my sisters. Blallen was like an older bachelor uncle to all of us, but the girls were somewhat like daughters to him. It was obvious he loved their attention and was happy for some relief from the headaches of contending with my cousins and me.

Wearing brand new store-bought dress-up clothing was a luxury during the Depression. The older Weaver girls were obsessed with a desire for one new dress to take back to college for the fall term. They surmised that Blallen had been saving his monthly pay for years and almost every nickel of his pay was in a savings account at the local bank. His only spending was for Prince Albert, his favorite pipe tobacco, and perhaps a new curved-stem pipe every three or four years. He only purchased a new pipe when the wooden bowl finally burned through on the old one. He always received Christmas gifts from family members consisting of new Big Smith overalls, flannel shirts, and new socks. He had no relatives or close friends to spend his money on so the girls reasoned that Blallen probably would be overjoyed to find some way to spend his "shekels" and they had plenty of suggestions for him.

Early in the summer, they began talking in Blallen's presence about going shopping in Dodge City, nearly forty-five miles northwest of the ranch. They imagined it as an exciting all-day trip plus the luxury of eating out in a restaurant. What a great time they would have together in the city. Doris and Vivian were masterful in conjuring up great images of the fun, excitement, and experiences they would have during the great shopping trip.

Their plan included going to the dress shop, trying on the latest fashions, and modeling each dress for Blallen. Blallen would be paying for the purchases so he was to be the judge and decide which dress he liked best on each of the girls. As the summer progressed, their slogan became, "Blallen, let's go shopping!"

Leaving the ranch chores and venturing off to the city was a new thought for Bill. He would need to take a bath, shave, and dress in his best overalls and shirt. He wasn't too sure about going to a strange place, being around women in a dress shop, and being on his best behavior. Gradually, Bill warmed up to the idea as he realized how grateful and pleased it would make the girls. He finally relented and agreed to take them shopping.

The big day for the exciting trip arrived. When Blallen and his entourage of Weaver girls reached Dodge City and entered the fancy dress shop, the girls were quick to introduce Mr. Allen to the head saleslady who promptly found a chair from which he could view the dress modeling process. The girls began modeling low-priced to mid-priced dresses but Mr. Allen didn't like their looks and insisted upon higher quality attire, much to the girls' delight. He seemed elated each time the saleslady referred to him as Mr. Allen. Mama later disclosed that one of Bill's desires in life was to be called "Mister" and not just as referred to as Bill. He always called Mama "The Missus" and Pop "The Mister."

Once the dresses were decided upon, Blallen would proudly produce his First State Bank checkbook to pay for the purchases. Years earlier, Mama helped him open a savings account and checking account in Mullinville, something he had never experienced, and then learned that he was practically illiterate and could barely sign his name. She taught him where to sign the check and assured him any storekeeper would gladly fill out a check for him and he needed only to sign it.

Doris, Vivian, Marjorie c.1933

After trying on dresses and modeling them for Blallen, everyone was hungry and ready for a nice meal at a restaurant. Blallen was the man of the hour and was encouraged to order whatever he wanted from the restaurant menu before the long drive back to Eagle Canyon Ranch. The girls raved and applauded him for his generosity and they would let admirers know Blallen had selected their new dresses. The summer shopping spree became an annual tradition and highlight for him. It was one of the few times he could do something to make his adopted Weaver girls so overjoyed and he gradually learned to relish being the center of attention on the trip.

Gradually, Bill was less like a hired hand and more like a favorite older uncle to the Weaver Five. He lived in the lower apartment at our house and had all his meals with the family. We dubbed Bill with a variety of nicknames and our favorite was Blallen. Bill always bought gifts for us at Christmas and we loved his generosity. We bragged on him that he was just like Santa or Santy and eventually it became another endearing nickname, Sandy-man.

Blissful are those who give without remembering
and receive without forgetting.

CHAPTER TWENTY-THREE

A Bully is Taught a Lesson

Grade school days in the 1930s were fun and carefree for most of us. Recess was exciting as we ran back and forth on the grass and dirt playground enjoying our favorite sport of "shinny." The game got its name because of the bruised, skinned shins received when an opposing player missed kicking the shinny ball and instead connected with another player's shin.

The eight-inch, red shinny ball was kicked back and forth, up and down the field. There was no goalie but the object was to kick the ball to the opponent's fence at the end of the field to ring up a score. If the shinny field happened to be wet or muddy, the girls would convince us boys to play their favorite games of Run-Sheep-Run or Drop the Handkerchief.

While these games were happening, a big, heavy kid we called Weenie was running around the playground to find some smaller boy to tease and pick on. Weenie received his nickname due to his appearance. He wore blue denim overalls that fit skin-tight over his fat thighs. They each looked like a plump wiener stuffed into his overalls.

Weenie would grab or chase down some little kid, pin him to the ground with his oversized body, and spit in his face. This usually resulted in the little kid crying and sobbing when Weenie let him up off the ground. Most of us just ignored Weenie and paid little attention to his actions. I suppose we wanted to let him know we didn't like his behaviors without actually confronting him. But secretly we each worried that Weenie was the biggest kid around and he might try to tackle us to give us the same treatment.

One day during afternoon recess, Weenie pinned down a good friend of Dorl Rader's which really riled up Dorl. He just couldn't let the attack on his friend go scot-free. Dorl knew none of us individually could pin Weenie since he probably weighed twice as much as the next biggest kid. But Dorl figured that as a group we could gang up on him. Dorl proposed to us that if we all teamed up we could dogpile Weenie and teach him a good lesson.

A few days later at recess, Dorl gave the signal and seven or eight of us all slammed into Weenie at the same time, knocking him to the ground. Before Weenie could get away, we started stacking our bodies one on another right on top of Weenie in a huge dogpile.

Dorl was near the bottom of the heap and yelled into Weenie's big ear, "If you pick on any kid smaller than you ever again, we'll pile on you even higher." Weenie was blubbering, crying, and gasping that he couldn't breathe and was about to die. After we all piled off, Weenie was wiping his tears and his runny nose with a big, red handkerchief he always carried in his back overalls pocket. He wasn't really hurt but he spent the rest of the recess sitting all by himself and whimpering.

We weren't sure if Weenie would tattle on us, but figured he couldn't tell on us without telling on himself. Our gang never heard a thing from any of the teachers about taking the matter into our own hands. The best ending to the scuffle was that Weenie never bullied anyone ever again.

The hardest thing to swallow is a dose of your own medicine.

CHAPTER TWENTY-FOUR

Salt Pork and Bull Durham

Louie Loveland was a good-hearted neighbor who was way too long on kids and bad luck, but way too short on good sense and income. The Loveland family lived twelve miles south of Mullinville on the Coldwater road. He had a hilly farm with hard clay soil where crops did poorly even in years with plenty of rainfall.

Pop always stopped to visit with Louie and the unique thing to me about Louie was his corncob pipe. None of our relatives smoked so I was intrigued by his pipe and his sack of Bull Durham smoking tobacco. I always watched with great interest as Louie would take his pocket knife, clean out the old ashes in his pipe, and then begin filling it with Bull Durham, the cheapest tobacco available. He filled his pipe with tobacco and packed it. While holding the pipe in one hand and the tobacco sack in the  other, he would grab the tobacco sack drawstring in his teeth, yank it closed, and then return the tobacco sack back into his overalls pocket. He lit a wooden kitchen match to get the tobacco burning and then puffed away. He was the first corncob pipe smoker I had ever seen, making quite an impression on me.

My dad felt sorry for the Lovelands when he heard they were scraping the bottom of the barrel for vittles. It reminded him of times when he went hungry as a child, growing up with a large family on a preacher's income. Pop would go visit Bill Sager who was proprietor of Sager's General Store and Grocery in Mullinville. Bill would finally agree that Pop could set up a big cardboard box in a back aisle of the store to collect food for the Lovelands. No customer left the store without hearing the plight of the Lovelands and nearly everybody put some canned goods, flour, or a sack of spuds in the box. When the food box was filled, Pop would load it into the back seat of the Chevy ready for the trip to the Loveland farmstead. Pop always took Lovelands a half-case of fresh eggs when our pullets started laying abundantly in the spring. Eighteen dozen eggs went a long way to feed a hungry family. Louie had pride, not wanting to admit that he accepted charity, so Pop would manage to tactfully get the donated food into the house to Mrs. Loveland who accepted it gratefully, many times to the point of tears.

Sometimes Louie's pride would get in the way and Pop would have to agree to trade fresh eggs, cream, and homemade butter for Louie's home-cured salt pork shoulders and bacon slabs. Mama always dreaded Pop coming home with Loveland's cured pork even though she appreciated the gesture. Morton's Sugar Cure was used a lot on pork in those days and it made the pork so salty that no insects or vermin would touch it. After being cured and stored in the smokehouse in barrels of oats, the meat was so dry and hard that we could pound a nail with a slab of Louie's bacon.

When Pop arrived home with the cured pork he had received in barter for eggs or cream, Mama would be faced with the weeklong task of soaking the tough, dry blocks of meat in crocks of water to lessen the salty taste and make it soft enough to slice and fry. Despite the effort, Pop reminded us never to waste food because of the times he went hungry as a child. We lived by the adage, "waste not, want not."

From Pop's visits, we all learned a lot about caring for others and sharing with neighbors who were having a struggle just to provide the necessities. It made us appreciate what we had a lot more when we realized how little they had in comparison.

Don't judge each day by the harvest you reap
but by the seeds that you plant. ~Robert Louis Stevenson

CHAPTER TWENTY-FIVE

Ice Cream that Wouldn't Melt

There was always great anticipation each spring as the school year came to a close and the city cousins looked forward their annual reunion at the ranch. It seemed their parents were as excited to send them off to the ranch for the summer as I was to have them around again. As we got older, we began to take everything in stride and were more able to fend for ourselves. Because of that, Mama got a vacation from her summer household chores and ranch duties to take Grandma Marriage to visit her relatives. Pop had ten brothers and sisters, and Mama had a passel of aunts, uncles, and cousins so there were plenty of kinfolk to go visit. Mama's trips were usually within a day's drive from the ranch, lasting for a week or ten days.

During Mama's absence, Blallen was the designated chief cook and bottle washer when my sisters weren't home from college. He fried all foods in lard or in bacon grease, giving the eggs and potatoes a great flavor. Homemade bread toast, freshly churned butter, and wild sand hill plum jelly topped off the meals. Pop never learned his way around the kitchen, so while Mama was gone we kids took turns doing the cooking, too.

We were taught at an early age that looking forward to a special occasion was half the enjoyment and fun of the affair. That feeling rubbed off from our folks who spent considerable time thinking, planning, and talking about a future activity. Ice cream night each Saturday was one such pleasurable occasion.

Saturday night was chosen because that was the day Tiny, the ice man, delivered ice from Coldwater, a town about twenty miles down the road south of the ranch. Tiny was a giant of a man from our waist-level vantage point. It amazed us kids to see him clamp those steel ice tongs onto a hundred pound chunk of ice and throw it over his shoulder. Tiny had a heavy, red rubber cape which kept his back from getting soaked as the ice melted while he carried it on a hot and sizzling summer day. He toted the chunk of ice to the big five-foot-tall icebox that was located in the front room of the ranch house because it was too big for the kitchen. Pop always ordered an extra fifty pound chunk of ice on Saturday to be used in freezing homemade ice cream.

Jack Clevenger drew the Saturday night ice cream mix making detail. He had seen Mama make a cooked custard ice cream base using egg yolks and corn starch as thickeners. Extra thick cream from the milk separator was saved to make the sweet, homemade ice cream especially good and rich. With his limited expertise and because he was always bragging about his abilities, Jack convinced us all that he was a whiz at making ice cream. We were so envious and so anxious to have our traditional ice cream night, in spite of Mama's absence, that we were more than willing to believe him.

About half-way through the normal cranking time with this marvelous mixture in the ice cream freezer, the crank suddenly got harder and harder to turn. Woolo and I had to trade off every twenty cranks, then every ten cranks until we played out and could crank no more. We couldn't figure out why it froze so fast, but the anticipation of a big bowl of ice cream after all that tough cranking was our main concern. We always packed the ice cream in the freezer by pouring off all the saltwater, pouring in more salt and ice, and then covering it with a blanket to hold it cold and firm until after supper.

That night at supper Jack was bragging about how great the ice cream would be when we served it. We opened the freezer lid to pull the paddle but it wouldn't budge no matter how hard we yanked and pulled. Finally, we were able to half-way dig and gouge the cold mixture out and decided that the ice cream looked like frozen bread or cookie dough. The flavor was alright but it sure was chewy, not to mention being cold and chewy.

We began quizzing Jack on his marvelous mixture's recipe. Finally, Jack fessed up to the possibility that he might have put two cups of cornstarch in the concoction instead of two tablespoons. We decided that you shouldn't always believe a braggart or that if you do, you may well be disappointed.

Two of the worst human flaws are lying and bragging.

CHAPTER TWENTY-SIX

Jocko and the Runaway Horse

୨୦୧

Excitement filled the air as the Eagle Canyon Ranch fall roundup approached. Over two hundred of the deep red Marriage Mulley cows were flanked by sleek, fat calves, unmindful of the fact they soon would be separated from their mothers at weaning time. Weaning calves permitted the cows to cease giving milk and begin building strength, stamina, and weight before the next calving time in early spring.

Pop gathered me and all the city cousins together and explained, "During this fall roundup every able-bodied cowboy and saddle horse will be needed to round up the entire herd from the large buffalo

grass pasture. With all the canyons, every ravine must be checked for cows and calves."

Eagle Lake pasture was the furthest pasture from the ranch house. The large lake was surrounded by eight hundred and forty acres. It was situated in a low-lying valley which caught runoff rainfall from hundreds of acres of grass land. This lake was a valuable asset at the ranch, providing year-round water for cattle in this large pasture.

Pop went on to explain, "We'll all scatter out in all directions riding to the outer perimeter of the pastures. Then we'll begin to gather up the cattle and herd them toward the main corral at the barns near the ranch house. Once in the corral, the cows and calves will be separated to begin the weaning process. The calves will be kept in the corral where water and sorghum fodder are available. We'll herd the cows to the adjoining pasture. They'll have plenty of buffalo grass there."

All regular ranch hands and their womenfolk knew they would be subjected to loud bawling as the cows and calves, miserable and feeling desolate at being separated, bellowed back and forth across the corral to one another. Old-time ranchers claimed that weaning calves in the dark of the moon greatly reduced the bawling and aided the adjustment to the traumatic separation.

The city cousins were excited about the roundup and felt mighty important to be considered able-bodied cowboys for this special event. Due to anticipation of the drive, everyone jumped out of bed bright and early to be on hand for the hearty ranch breakfast. Mama, or Aunt Etta to the cousins, had prepared a he-man breakfast of fried eggs, sage sausage, fried potatoes, and home-made toast generously covered with home-churned butter. Delicious wild sand hill plum jelly was an added treat.

Stuffed with chow, the crew headed for the horse barn to saddle up. There was one big hitch. We were short one horse. I was slated to

ride Lightning, a black and white horse with a jagged white streak down his left side, much like a lightning bolt. Pop always rode his favorite, Old Roan, a strawberry roan with a blaze face. So that left Jack

Jack Clevenger on Witt, Eldon on Lightning

Clevenger without a horse. My brother, who was five years older than I, was working for a neighbor so his horse, Witt, was available. Long before the roundup, Kenny had made Pop promise that his little brother was never allowed to ride Witt. He claimed Witt was too high spirited for me to control. However, Kenny never dreamed Pop would even consider letting a greenhorn city cousin ride his prized horse.

Knowing Witt was a spirited horse, Uncle Benny began quizzing Jack about his riding skills. Since Jack considered himself the hero of every escapade, he told Pop he had ridden many times. He didn't let on that his riding experience was limited to riding ponies tied to an exercise wheel and walking in a circle at an amusement park in Wichita.

It took a while for us greenhorns to saddle up. Just getting a bridle on each horse was quite an ordeal for inexperienced cowboys especially when some ornery ranch horses resisted having the bridle-bit inserted between their teeth. Once bridled, the saddle blankets and saddles were thrown on and cinched up. Pop checked each cinch for tightness since the two older mares had a bad habit of blowing out their bellies to resist the heavy, tight cinching. "Looks like we're all set," Pop remarked after completing the check. Then Pop instructed everyone to mount up.

High-spirited and giddy, Witt began circling each time Jack attempted to put his foot in the stirrup to mount. This frustrated Jack nearly to exasperation. The last thing Jack wanted to do was request assistance. Pop was forced to grab Witt's bridle-bit and hold him steady while Jack mounted and positioned both feet in the stirrups and then settled himself in the saddle. Pop advised, "Above all, Jack, keep a tight rein on Witt and never, never let him have his head."

Pop had no more than straddled Old Roan when we heard a clatter of hooves and turned just in time to see Witt, with Jack astride, dashing through the corral gate. Pop shouted, "Jack, tighten up your reins and keep a hand tight on the saddle horn—above all don't fall off!" In a split second, Witt was up to breakneck speed, dashing down the half-mile lane to the old schoolhouse corner. Jack was so startled and so engrossed in gripping the saddle horn that he completely dropped both reigns. This startled Witt and gave him more momentum. Jack panicked. He wailed in a loud voice, "Uncle Benny, save me!"

Pop shouted for all of us to dismount, drop our reins, and run for the car parked in the barnyard. We raced for the old '29 Chevy, piled inside, on the front fenders, and on the running boards. We looked like a scene out of the Keystone Kops. Pop raced the motor and sped through the gate and down the lane.

The chase was on. He hoped to cut off Witt and Jack before they reached the open gate at the schoolhouse corner. The old flivver was no match for the spirited Witt who beat us there. The runaway horse rounded the schoolhouse corner with a terrified Jack still in the saddle. As luck would have it, Witt veered off the main country road and raced into a freshly plowed wheat field north of the road. His hooves sunk deeply into the soft soil with each step which pulled him down considerably, reducing his speed. In no time, Witt was exhausted.

As we were making our fast car ride Pop explained, "That was a lucky break. Our best chance to halt the runaway is to trap him in the corral. When he comes to a halt we'll spread out in a huge circle and head Witt and Jack toward the corral." Pop stood on the brakes and came to a fast stop. We all leaped out, ran into the plowed field, and formed a circular human chain nearly a quarter mile across. As Witt made a big loop in the plowed field, we all waved our straw hats, whooped, and hollered which directed Witt straight through the corral opening. Quickly we slammed the heavy wooden gate closed to prevent his escape.

The lathered, panting horse carrying a trembling, terrified rider was a sight to behold. Jack's face was white from the terror. He hated to admit he needed assistance but Pop had to practically pry Jack's hands from the saddle horn. Pop was so relieved Jack had not fallen off Witt or worse yet, could have been dragged to his death by a foot caught in a stirrup. Instead of the reprimand he had in mind, Pop turned it into praise. As he unknotted Jack's clenched hands from the saddle horn, he proclaimed, "Jack, you were an amazing sight. That was a magnificent ride and the fastest ride ever witnessed on Eagle Canyon Ranch!" With tears streaming down his chunky, sweating face, Jack beamed with pride but was speechless. From that day forth he was known as "Jocko the Magnificent." Needless to say, the big roundup was delayed several hours.

The runaway episode taught Jocko and each of us a valuable lesson. Be aware of the dangers when you take a risk, especially when experience and skill is required.

> Sometimes it's better to look back and say,
> "I can't believe I did that," than to say,
> "I wish I had done that."

CHAPTER TWENTY-SEVEN

Threshing Days

Blazing sun and hot, dry August winds set the stage for threshing days at Eagle Canyon Ranch. Before the introduction of the combine, cereal grains were harvested with a binder pulled by a mule team or tractor. As wheat or oats stalks were clipped off by the sharp sickle, they fell onto a moving slotted canvas which carried them to the knotter that securely bound each bundle with binder twine. The bundles were dropped off the binder platform in piles, later to be stood nearly upright in tepee-shaped shocks for drying and curing.

Every able-bodied cousin and ranch hand was involved in shocking. It was a hot, scratchy task, but necessary to dry the grain and foliage prior to the threshing process. The gang of cousins, ranging in age from nine to sixteen, was finally getting old enough to help rather than be in the way. Once the bundles were dry, it was time for threshing. We cousins felt pretty important riding in the bundle wagons, arranging dry bundles as they were forked onto the wagon, and then tramping them down to permit a larger load to be hauled to the threshing machine.

Threshing Days

The exciting time for us was the day the custom threshing machine and huge steam engine chugged onto the ranch. They were ready to thresh the grain and blow the remaining chopped straw through a long twelve-inch diameter tube, creating a tall stack of straw. Threshing machines were too expensive for the average farmer to own, hence, a custom thresher was available for hire, moving from ranch to farm throughout the entire community. Some threshers charged by the bushel or by the day if grain yields were poor.

Fall threshing time united neighbors as they worked side by side as a workforce, following the threshing machine as it was moved from farm to farm. Each farmer brought his horse or mule team, farm hands, and bundle wagon to help in the joint effort of hauling the shocks of grain from the field to the threshing machine. Most of all, a large crew of bundle pitchers was needed. A steady stream of bundles must be pitched off the bundle wagons onto the huge, moving conveyer belt to keep the threshing machine running full blast without interruption.

Jellybean Sherman, the local custom thresher, loudly insisted on a steady flow of bundles to be elevated up the conveyer belt into the straw walkers. He would nearly have a spasm if the thresher was allowed to run dry, claiming the thresher would beat itself to death with no  straw to cushion the mechanism. Jellybean had a short fuse, well known by most of the bundle pitchers, and periodically, they would set the stage to experience his explosive reaction. Some fellows were aggravated by his temperament, in addition to the fact that Jellybean had a comfortable seat under the sunshade of his big steam engine while everyone else toiled in the sun. Sometimes he even dozed while the bundle pitchers were working vigorously and exposed to the dry, scorching wind.

About mid-morning, Bud Beckett would give the signal to slug the machine. The bundle pitchers would immediately pitch twice as fast as usual, causing a huge volume of bundles to be carried up the conveyer at once, choking the mechanism. This caused the stalled machine to throw the huge belt off the steam engine drive pulley. The sudden change of engine racket would jolt Jellybean from his nap to consciousness. Shouting an obscenity, he would throw his eight-pound sledge hammer into the air to relieve some of his anger. All hands knew to stand clear when Jellybean erupted.

It was a big chore to get the twelve-inch-wide and fifty-foot-long conveyor belt back on the pulleys. The job entailed unblocking the twelve-foot-tall steam engine wheels and slowly moving it closer to the thresher to allow slack for placing the heavy continuous belt back on both pulleys. Once in place, Jellybean, sweating profusely, would throw the engine into reverse until the belt was the proper tension, then block the wheels again to prevent creeping. All during this lengthy procedure, the crews could rest under the shade of the bundle wagon, chuckling over their prank. Resting ended the moment Jellybean yelled, "Pitch bundles," as the thresher came to life again.

Various farm hands pulled pranks on each other during the busy threshing season. One favorite was to strip a piece of volunteer sorghum cane, then throw it toward any hand who was known to be deathly afraid of snakes, yelling "snake" as it flew toward him. This caused some fast action and often swearing as well.

One of the pleasures of threshing days for us youngsters was partaking of the huge, delicious dinners prepared by the various farm women and their daughters. It seemed each cook was trying to outdo her neighbors by preparing a bountiful meal. Tender meat choices, mashed potatoes and gravy, hot bread with home-churned butter, and garden-fresh vegetables were topped off by pie or cake, covered with rich, whipped cream. The feast made us forget the hot, itchy wheat fields.

Mrs. Burrton and her daughters were great cooks and specialized in crispy fried chicken from their free-ranging home grown flock. During the noon meal at their farm, Mrs. Burrton remarked, "Men, we would have had even more fried chicken but Charlie ran out of shotgun shells!" Her remark drew a hearty laugh from the hungry crew.

Mrs. Thach and her daughter, Ruth, were near neighbors. Their specialty was meaty, cream-roasted chicken from their flock of large, White Rock capons. What a tender, delicious treat for everyone. Although we often griped about the discomfort and heat of threshing days, the entertaining experiences and tasty meals far exceeded our complaints.

After a day of threshing, there were huge straw stacks, sometimes thirty feet tall, left in the wheat fields. They provided a fun place for us cousins to dig tunnels and play on a cool evening after ranch work ceased. While we younger boys played in the straw, Dux, Jocko, and L. J. headed off to the barn. Jocko had a pack of Kool cigarettes that he smuggled to the ranch from Wichita. Pop and Mama highly disapproved of smoking and drinking alcohol, so the ornery, older boys tried to keep it a secret from us. But, they couldn't contain their boasting about sneaking a smoke and even tried to get us to take a puff. Those who did immediately knew they didn't like the burning sensation in their mouths and throats. It brought back the distasteful memory of smoking catalpa pods with Kenny and Marilyn. Somehow we knew it was a bad habit to be avoided.

Doing anything worthwhile requires work. The only thing that ever sat its way to success was a hen.

CHAPTER TWENTY-EIGHT

The Incredible Race

The late-summer sun shone brightly at Eagle Canyon Ranch as my older brother, Kenny, and our cousin, Marilyn Marriage, and I were dawdling and loafing at the ranch house, pondering what to do with ourselves on such a fine day. They were both fourteen years old and I was nine so it was their responsibility to look after me and keep me company. Our folks and Marilyn's parents, Uncle Ira and Aunt Frances, were away visiting friends in Greensburg that Sunday afternoon.

Of course, at their ages, the typical ranch activities such as horseback riding, hiking in the canyons, or swimming in the huge livestock water tank were of no interest to them. They were both known to be the impish trouble-makers of their families and had a history of getting each other into hot water. Egg-throwing, getting sick on green peaches, and almost drowning in the water tank were just of few of their previous escapades. However, Marilyn, the eternal instigator, decided they needed some excitement while her parents and her bossy older siblings, Lawrence and Lois, were away.

As we were lounging in the shade of the summer house, Marilyn spied our family car, a 1929 Chevy sedan and her father's car, a 1929 Chevy two-door parked in front of the ranch house. Suddenly, out of boredom, she remarked, "Why don't we have a car race to decide which is the fastest Chevy? We can each drive a car and race against one another."

Kenny was a bit reluctant since his job was to look after me that afternoon, but Marilyn had a way of persisting and convincing him to take part in her hair-brained schemes. After a few minutes of hemming and hawing, Kenny agreed to the idea. The keys were always left in the ignition, so the cars were just sitting there, tempting both of them with the thrill of a great race. The more they thought about the idea, the more it seemed like fun and excitement.

Like most farm boys and farm girls in that day, Kenny had been driving in the fields and pastures since he was a "little shaver" of ten or eleven years old. Marilyn was a city girl from Wichita and had little, if any, driving experience. She barely knew how to use the clutch to shift gears. Secretly, she probably envied her country cousins who were allowed to drive to town with their parents. And she had heard her older brother's stories of driving the cousins to school in town years ago after the country school on the ranch was closed.

Marilyn thought she needed some company in her car, so she grabbed me and put me in the front seat next to her while Kenny jumped into Pop's Chevy sedan. Both car engines were started and hitting on all six cylinders when Kenny instructed, "We'll drive up the lane to the main county road before starting the race."

Kenny led the way as we followed him to the main road where the two Chevys could be positioned side-by-side to begin the race. We were the only family living along the dirt road and, fortunately, Sunday afternoon traffic was scarce and posed no real problem. Kenny directed Marilyn to stay abreast of his car until both cars were in high gear. He would then honk his car horn to indicate the beginning of the big race. That was the signal to "put the pedal to the metal."

The exciting race began. Both cars were roaring and smoking and soon reached the break-neck speed of thirty-five miles an hour. Big clouds of dust billowed behind the speeding cars as we thundered down the bumpy gravel road. As Marilyn swerved and careened down the road, she kept looking over at me and yelling, "Isn't this fun, Eldon?" I was beginning to realize we were going awfully fast and started shrieking in terror for Marilyn to slow down.

We were approaching a rather sharp curve in the road and Kenny was in the lead by that time. He slowed down to make the turn, but Marilyn, being an inexperienced driver, failed to cut her speed. When she realized her mistake and in her effort to negotiate the turn, she slammed on the brakes and slid across the road into the opposite ditch in front of Art and Fred Lutz's place. As the wheels dropped into the ditch, the big, heavy car flipped over on its side and continued to slide several yards before the engine died.

With the sudden bouncing and lurching, I felt myself go airborne and when I opened my eyes, I was sprawled in the back seat while Marilyn clung to the steering wheel for dear life. It was several minutes until we realized that neither of us was hurt. Kenny made the turn and continued down the road until he noticed we weren't behind him. Realizing that something was wrong, he turned around and drove back to the scene of our accident. He helped us out of the wrecked car and we sat in the ditch to calm down. Once he determined we both were alright, the next concern was how to get both cars back to the ranch house. Since we didn't have permission to be driving, it was part of the plan to have both cars parked back at the ranch when the folks arrived at home as though nothing had happened.

Kenny shouted, "I'll go get Blallen to bring the tractor over to pull your Chevy out of the ditch. Just wait here for us." Marilyn and I were more than willing to wait in the shade of the upturned car while we regained our wits after the wild ride into the ditch.

Our faithful hired hand was relaxing in the shade of the summer house in the front yard when Kenny sped down the lane. Blallen enjoyed sitting in the shade and smoking his pipe filled with his favorite Prince Albert tobacco when our parents weren't around. Kenny jumped out of the car, waving and running toward Blallen to explain the situation. The old John Deere tractor and plow was parked nearby at the barn. Blallen unhitched the plow and followed Kenny to the scene of the accident. We were cheered to hear the pop, pop, pop, of the old Johnny-pop tractor and see Blallen chugging our way at the amazing speed of five miles an hour. When he arrived, all we could hear from Blallen was his muttering and grumbling about dumb kids always getting themselves into trouble.

Blallen sized up the situation and edged the tractor close to the stranded car. Being on its side, the front axle was sticking up in the air so Blallen hooked a heavy log chain onto the tractor drawbar and the other end of the chain to the front axle of the Chevy. Blallen continued to grumble and then shouted angrily, "Get back you kids! Both them tires are fixin' to blow out when this thing comes crashing down."

Blallen revved up the tractor and it gave out a loud pop, pop, pop, as it moved slowly forward. The old Chevy groaned and without warning came lumbering down onto all four wheels. The dust settled and the car stopped shaking. Fortunately, the tires survived the impact. Blallen moved the log chain to the front bumper and towed the car out of the ditch and back onto the gravel road.

The drive home was much calmer and more to my liking as we putted along at fifteen miles an hour. I could hear Marilyn sobbing and lamenting, "What will Papa do to me when he sees the scratched paint and dents on his car?" I was still shaking in my boots, just happy to be alive, and not really concerned about being punished.

Upon arrival at the ranch house, Kenny told Marilyn to park the car so the damaged side was in the shade near the three-car garage. There was considerable damage to the radiator and front fender, too. They were both trying to figure out when might be the best time to tell her father about the accident.

Our parents returned and soon we were eating supper in the dining room of the ranch house. Kenny and Marilyn glanced at each other nervously throughout the meal, but no one seemed to catch on to their unusual, subdued behavior. I had been instructed not to say anything about my wild adventure with them. Blallen was his usual quiet self. After supper, we sat in the big parlor visiting. Marilyn's conscience began to get the best of her as she waited until it appeared that Uncle Ira was in a jovial mood so she could break the news about the car. She knew it would be better to admit to what she had done rather than have it found out later by her papa.

"Papa," she began slowly and then started to sob, "I need to talk to you about something. We need to go outside." Ira was caught off-guard and truly concerned about his youngest daughter's weeping. They went outside and she went on, "It seems that something has happened to the car."

Ira seemed surprised and replied, "What do you mean?"

"Well, it seems to have some scratches and dents in it," she went on. She continued to sob and tell the horrifying story about sliding across the road and crashing into the ditch, but leaving out the part about the big race which led up to the accident. To further soften his reaction she suggested, "I think my punishment should be that I can't drive the car for a whole month."

After seeing all the damage and hearing the car was on its side in the ditch, Ira was relieved that neither of us was injured. Fortunately for Marilyn, he merely reprimanded her for driving the family car without proper driver's training and for driving without his permission. She was not to let this happen again. Kenny was also reprimanded by Pop Weaver for speeding and for agreeing with Marilyn to be involved. From the incredible race, both learned another lesson about thinking of the risks of their behaviors before taking action on wild ideas.

The trouble with trouble is that it always starts out as fun.

CHAPTER TWENTY-NINE

Sheepherder on a Cattle Ranch

The terrible drought of the Dust Bowl dragged on. Dust storms, drought, jackrabbits, and grasshoppers caused crop failures plus poor prices nearly ruined most farmers. When cattle pastures dried up, many ranchers were forced to sell their cowherds, often for fifteen or twenty dollars per head or less. Government programs were instituted to limit crop production and those who participated were guaranteed a certain price for their crops. Pop resisted the programs as long as he could since he did not want to take a handout from the government. He thought it was a poorly conceived idea to pay men not to work and to fix prices. He reasoned that the price the government offered was so low that we'd be better off keeping our livestock rather than selling it for practically nothing. At least we would have something to eat. Many ranchers and farmers took the deal since money was so scarce and any means of generating a little cash was welcomed.

Pop had faith it would eventually rain so each September he continued to plant wheat by dusting it into the soil and praying for a rain in the fall to perform the miracle of germination. One very unusual rainy fall in 1937 produced a tremendous growth of winter wheat that was wonderful for livestock grazing. Through a neighbor, Pop got the name of a Texas sheep rancher offering cash for grazing five thousand head of woolies. What a wonderful opportunity to finally have some cash flow. Pop called the rancher on the old oak wall telephone and a deal was struck.

The following week several huge double-decker semi-trailers arrived at Eagle Canyon Ranch with five thousand bleating, hungry lambs. Pop guided the drivers to the big eight hundred and forty acre north wheat field. An additional trucker arrived with a portable corral, much like snow fence, to serve as a nighttime holding pen for protection from coyotes. Behind his truck was a portable sheepherder's hut. It was a one room eight-foot by sixteen-foot hut equipped with a thirty-inch-wide wooden bunk. The bunk was on one wall of the hut and covered by two old blankets. A small cast iron, flat top, coal burning Topsy stove served both for cooking and warming the hut. A Mexican sheepherder, Romero, who barely spoke English, completed the total unit. He had a box of paperback books in Spanish. On one wall he had a kerosene lantern and pegs to hang his coats and hat. On another peg was a big string of dried chili peppers.

Romero had two shepherd dogs who shared his hut on cold nights. They were well-trained and could move the entire flock where desired just by commands from Romero.

One chilly fall day about a week after the sheep arrived, Pop and I rode horses up to the north wheat field and directly to Romero's hut. He spotted us coming, waved, and showed a wide smile just to see other human beings. The big Texas rancher had informed Pop that fresh eggs were the food item most missed by Romero. He smiled even more when Pop unloaded a whole batch of carefully packed fresh eggs from behind the saddle.

Romero waved for us to join him in his hut. It was nearly noon  when we arrived. He had a big kettle simmering on the Topsy stove and called it lamb chili. "You eat?" he asked. Pop never turned down food so we were soon seated on two wooden stools. Romero dished each of us a tin bowl of lamb chili. The tender chunks of lamb gave it a great aroma. We each took a big bite and an almost instantly thought we were on fire. Pop gasped and exclaimed, "Heavenly days. I need water!" Romero filled two tin cups out of his water pail and we managed to quench the burn and stop gasping. He was chuckling and smiling broadly at our antics but kept on eating heartily. We decided he must have put a whole string of chili peppers in that lamb chili. We would take a bite of chili then quickly wash it down. It was the first time I ever saw Pop violate the clean-your-plate rule.

During the winter we continued delivering eggs to Romero, but avoided being there anywhere near meal times. It seemed to me that being a sheepherder would be one of the loneliest jobs ever imaginable with only his two dogs as company for weeks on end.

The sheep made a great weight gain with very little death loss and none by coyotes. The rancher was pleased with loads of marketable, fat lambs and Pop felt like a millionaire with the cash payment after a long dry spell of no cash income on the ranch.

Whatever you are, be a good one. ~Abraham Lincoln

CHAPTER THIRTY

The Great Goddard Blizzard

Severe snowstorms and raging blizzards were common on the plains of Kansas. Shortages of trees and lack of shelterbelts permitted the strong, snowy wind to blow full force across the flat, barren plains. The only obstruction was fence rows full of tumbleweeds that caused dangerous snowdrifts to form across roadways and highways.

On a cold but clear January morning when I was ten years old, my dad and I left Eagle Canyon Ranch with a stock truck loaded with Marriage Mulley steers to be marketed at the huge stockyards in Wichita. Such trips with my dad were always exciting, not only due to seeing hundreds of cattle in the yards, but also to hear Pop visit with the commission men who sold and bought cattle for a per cent of the total business transaction. Rieff-King was Pop's favorite commission company especially since Mr. King would treat us to a big steak dinner in the Stockman's Steakhouse. Eating out at a restaurant in those days was a real treat in itself.

We always stayed all night with Grandfather William Ritter Weaver, retired from the Methodist Church ministry, and residing in a modest home at 316 South Oak Street west of the Arkansas River in Wichita. Aunt Winifred, one of Pop's younger sisters, lived with Grandfather Weaver, cooked his meals, and tended to his elderly needs. Following breakfast was hymn sing and prayer time. Aunt

Winnie accompanied us on the piano as we all joined in on favorite hymns. Pop always knew to allow an extra half hour for a departure time due to Grandfather's lengthy prayers which included our safe journey, the afflicted, the oppressed, the deprived, the homeless, the orphans, and the hungry children in faraway lands.

While in Wichita, Pop always made a pork sausage purchase at Eli Rush's Left Ham Sausage Meat Market. Eli theorized that since most hogs always lay on their right ham, it was stronger and tougher and therefore the left ham was more tender. Eli only used the left ham in his original Left Ham Sage Sausage. The family market slogan was "There is always a Rush at Eli's." Pop always enjoyed a visit with the proprietor prior to making a five pound sausage purchase.

We began our westward journey back to Eagle Canyon Ranch, watching for the cheapest gasoline in the city enroute. A light snow began falling and the bitter north wind increased as we left the city limits. With each mile, the flakes became larger and wetter, sticking to the highway and decreasing visibility. Pop was concerned and even thought of returning to Grandfather Weaver's until the storm subsided, but continued on our journey since we needed to get back to the ranch to feed the hungry cowherd. We had no way of knowing that eight to ten inches of snow with heavy drifting had been predicted.

Soon our old windshield wipers were coated with heavy, wet and freezing snow making the wipers sluggish and inadequate. Small drifts of snow began accumulating on the highway and the narrow shoulders were becoming snow covered making it difficult to see the edge of the highway. Pop decided we would pull in at the first town and wait out the blustery gale. Minutes ticked by as we drove more and more slowly into the oncoming storm while trying to avoid slipping off the road. Taillights of cars and trucks ahead of us became a guide through the blinding snow.

Suddenly, the brake lights of a pickup truck ahead of us glowed brightly as it and the cars ahead all came to a halt. We decided to keep the engine and heater running for warmth. Soon drifts were knee deep between vehicles. Suddenly our truck engine sputtered and died. The raging snow had blown through the hood vents and shorted out the distributor. Our windshield and side windows were already blanketed by the heavy, blinding snow. We sat there in the cold wondering what to do.

We were surprised by a pounding noise on the driver side window of the truck. A burly man coated with snow shouted, "The highway is blocked ahead with a semi-trailer jack-knifed across road. You'll have to walk a half-mile to Goddard." Then, he went on. We buttoned our coats tightly and climbed out onto the drifts, holding hands as we lunged through waist high snow. Pop and I struggled past numerous stalled trucks and cars already evacuated, joining more stranded motorists doing the same. Visibility was near zero as we struggled through more drifts. At my age and size, Goddard seemed miles away. Finally, we spotted a two-pump gasoline station already filled with stranded motorists. A large crowd had accumulated due to so many people traveling Highway 54, the main east to west corridor through southwest Kansas.

Soon, a man with a loud voice announced that the high school was open to all stranded individuals and to follow him south to the school. We all began trudging in a steady stream to the warm, well-lighted gymnasium. Everyone shook off all the snow possible from clothing and shoes, hoping in no time to be dried off and warm. The cafeteria had tables and seating. The huge padded mats lining the walls underneath the  basketball goals were soon spread out on the gym floor for make-shift sleeping quarters that night.

Ben Weaver never met a stranger and immediately began visiting and getting acquainted with fellow travelers in the cafeteria. Soon, a large group of listeners became involved. Pop capitalized upon the occasion and began explaining the important issues confronting the Kansas Legislature and affecting all Kansans. He had served in the Kansas House of Representatives starting in 1927 and was well-versed on the issues. Pop presented both the pros and cons of each proposed House Bill before soliciting opinions of the diverse group of stranded travelers. All were more knowledgeable at the conclusion of his discussion.

Meanwhile, a mixed group of young people found a loose basketball and soon had an intramural basketball game going on one end of the court. Gym lights were dimmed at ten o'clock as weary people stretched out on the mats, hoping to get some rest.

Morning sunlight and dwindling winds greeted the crowd of hungry travelers. The Goddard Market sold completely out of bread, canned meat, produce, and peanut butter. It was their largest sales in recent weeks. Snowplow crews worked throughout the night and broke through deep drifts to clear one lane from Wichita to  Goddard, a distance of fifteen miles. A local winch truck driver towed snow-buried vehicles out of the drifts over into the cleared lane on the highway. Soon a steady stream of traffic slowly drove toward Wichita. We returned to Grandfather Weaver's to spend an additional night until 54 Highway was opened on toward Pratt. Telephone lines were down preventing us from phoning the ranch and informing Mama of our whereabouts. Although this was troubling to Pop, he knew she would be confident we had taken refuge from the storm.

The following morning we began the one hundred and twenty mile trip back to Eagle Canyon Ranch, taking most of the day due to the one lane highway and slippery stretches of ice and snow. That evening a warm ranch house and a caring family welcomed us home from our tiring experience. We knew it could have been much worse if we had been stranded on the way to Wichita with the load of valuable steers or involved in a pile-up on the highway. We were grateful to be home safe and sound despite the snow delay.

There is no such thing in anyone's life as an unimportant day.
~Alexander Woollcott

CHAPTER THIRTY-ONE

My Baby Chick Enterprise

After earning money for my Montgomery Ward pocket watch and time went by, my wants exceeded my means. I needed another money-making project. When there was work I could do on the ranch, my pay of ten cents a day didn't go very far. Ray Thach, an older neighbor kid, had done well raising baby chicks. Chicks could be ordered by mail and those fuzzy little rascals were shipped to the post office. One hundred day-old chicks could be sent from the hatchery in a big chick shipping box. Mrs. Bryan, the Mullinville postmistress, phoned the families as soon as the chicks arrived to speed up getting them delivered. They needed to be fed and watered and the constant chirping in the mailroom nearly drove her bonkers.

Mama read a hatchery ad in *Capper's Weekly* advertising Buff Orpington chicks ready for immediate shipment, straight run, for only four dollars and ninety-five cents per hundred chicks. The pullets could be saved for layers and the roosters could be butchered for delicious fried chicken. In the same newspaper were plans for a homemade chick battery designed to house one hundred chicks from hatchlings to six weeks, ready for the big chicken house. The battery ads pictured little chicks poking their heads through the poultry wire and pecking away at the feed in troughs on the outside supports. This got me even more excited about the possibilities.

My parents knew I didn't have enough money to order the chicks or buy the starter mash and grain needed, so we worked out a business deal. They had been buying pullets from a neighbor to put in the laying house. They would purchase pullets from me if I promised to do all the feeding, watering, and cleaning the chick battery. They'd pay for the chicks and feed up front and later this amount would be taken out of my payment for the pullets. To me, that seemed like a good deal but a long wait for earnings. Amazingly, the time flew by.

Blallen said he reckoned he could help me build the battery while I waited on the chick order. He had especially good skills at rough carpentry and could make or repair almost anything around the ranch. Stacks of large-dimension lumber were salvaged from the big shed that collapsed during the terrible, destructive cyclone of 1934. Corral fence was built from two-foot by eight-foot lumber and always needed replacing when cattle or the weather caused damage. Blallen constructed heavy two-foot by one-foot salt boxes for the cattle as well. The most helpful project Blallen ever did for me was to build that four-tier chick battery for brooding day-old baby chicks.

My part of the battery building project was to straighten and hammer back all the nails from the salvaged shed lumber we selected for the project. I spent most of two days pulling nails with the nail bar just getting the lumber cleaned for sawing. There wasn't much conversation as we worked and Blallen needed a break every so often to puff on his pipe. But, it was really exciting as I helped Blallen saw, nail, bolt, and assemble the four-tier battery. Each tier had its own dropping tray, a feeder, and a waterer for the chicks to eat and drink. Blallen reckoned we'd have the battery built long before the chicks' arrival.

He allowed space between each deck for runners to slide the metal dropping trays in and out. He warned me I might get mighty tired of cleaning those trays but I'd probably live through the ordeal. We put the feed and water troughs on the outside shelves. Finally, we were ready for the chicks.

A small room on the ground floor of the ranch house seemed to be ideal for the chick battery as it already had a butane gas heating stove to keep the room cozy during the cold winter months. From the *Book of Knowledge* we learned that baby chicks need eighty degree temperature and fifty percent humidity for best health and growth.

Cooler temperature causes them to pile up trying to keep warm, causing suffocation.

At last, we mailed an order for one hundred chicks from a Clinton, Missouri hatchery which guaranteed one hundred percent live delivery. They were shipped in boxes of one hundred; twenty-five chicks in each of four compartments. Amazingly, a newly hatched baby chick can survive over forty-eight hours without food or water. The hatchery often sent an extra chick in each section to replace any chick that failed to survive the long, rattling and rough railroad ride.

Nearly a week later the old oak wall telephone rang three longs and a short ring. It was Mrs. Bryan phoning from the post office that the chicks had arrived and must be picked up as soon as possible, and most certainly before five o'clock. She declared, "Their loud peeping is driving me to distraction here at the post office!" Soon after Mrs. Bryan's call, we whizzed to Mullinville in the old Chevy, sometimes reaching the break-neck speed of forty-five miles an hour, but it seemed so much longer than usual to me. I was so anxious to see my dreams come true.

Mrs. Bryan gave us receipts to sign before we loaded the carton of chirping chicks into the car. They were now more than ready for food and water after a long railroad trip. Mrs. Bryan was so relieved when we departed with our load. Enroute home, the loud chirping and peeping of a hundred chicks made us realize how much she endured.

Blallen helped me carry the carton to the brooder room. Unloading the tiny, soft yellow chicks was really a treat. Blallen helped me lift the fuzzy little boogers, as I sweetly called them, out of the shipping box. I carefully placed them into the top deck of the battery which was the warmest spot for the new babies. Each chick immediately began pecking at the mash, dipping their bills in the fresh water, and chirping happily between pecks. I was overjoyed and even the ever-doubtful Blallen seemed to be pleased with our project.

It was amazing how rapidly they grew each week and started adding feathers. As chicks develop and age, less heat is needed and they can be moved down to lower tiers to allow the chicks more headroom and space. Soon I had room for a new shipment of chicks. Weeks flew by and before long forty-six pullets and forty-five roosters were ready to be moved to the henhouse in the barnyard.

I kept a record of the mash, pellets, and scratch grain to be subtracted from the sale of the pullets. When I settled up with my parents, I had more spending money than I ever imagined. I could hardly wait to order another batch of baby chicks. The  chick enterprise taught me responsibility and reliability because their lives depended upon my efforts to keep them warm, fed, and watered every day of the week.

The difference between try and triumph is a little umph.

CHAPTER THIRTY-TWO

The Wedding Present

One sunny day in 1938, a skinny, scruffy-coated black and white dog wandered into the barnyard. He looked half-starved so I filled a pan with warm milk for him at the cow barn. He was very hesitant and skittish, even about approaching the milk, which made me think some mean person had abused him.

I named him Duke although he was a far cry from resembling royalty. It was nearly three days before Duke would permit anyone to get close enough to pet him. He gradually began trusting me and within a week he became a friendly, happy dog. Then, I got out the horse curry comb and removed the trash and spiny cockle burrs from his matted fur. He began putting weight on his thin frame and soon began to look fit and healthy.

Duke appeared to be a Border collie mix and seemed to enjoy the cattle and horses. He would trot along beside me as I rode Toots into the north pasture each evening to drive the cows in for milking. As Pop always instructed me, it was just dandy to trot Toots out to the pasture to where the cows were grazing, but I was to ride slowly as I herded the cows back to the barn. Their udders full of milk couldn't take a trot back to the cow barn. However, Duke's natural herding instinct came into play when a lagging milk cow needed to be nudged along.

After a few weeks I noticed as I brushed him that Duke was developing a very fat belly. I wanted to make him presentable when wedding guests arrived for Vivian's wedding. She came home from college a week early to finish her wedding preparations. The big event was to be held at the ranch with Grandfather William Weaver, a Methodist pastor, performing the ceremony.

Naturally, I introduced Vivian to Duke. She almost immediately informed me that Duke should be renamed Duchess as she saw that my dog was soon going to deliver a litter of puppies. It never dawned on me that all the weight my dog was gaining could be puppies. I was amazed and excited about the prospect of more puppies.

A few days later, Duchess failed to show up to help me bring in the milk cows. I began searching and calling for Duke and finally heard a sharp, loud bark in response. She had found a cool spot in

the old, abandoned ice cave in the canyon south of the house where she gave birth to her family. It was a sight to behold. There were eleven whimpering, squirming puppies, all black and white like Duchess. I climbed down the canyon bank with bread and milk for her. And I was sure she would be hungry for a cottontail rabbit we had shot the night before during our hunting adventure in our wheat pasture. Duchess was mighty hungry after her ordeal and eagerly wolfed down her meal.

Vivian laughed and joked with the wedding guests saying, "Little Eldon had one dog yesterday, and today he has twelve dogs." News of this birth created quite a stir among the visiting family and friends. Kenny teased me about the excitement for several days chanting, "One day, one dog. Wedding day, twelve dogs."

The little cute puppies grew rapidly as they put on more fur and finally opened their eyes to view their littermates and the world around them. Watching them grow and change was so exciting. It was amazing to me as a young boy that the puppies soon began roaming around the outside of their ice cave den. In a few days, they were romping and playing like a group of school children at recess. As weaning time approached, Pop informed me there was no way we could feed and care for eleven puppies. He decided I could keep my favorite of the litter, but we had to find homes for the remaining ten pups.

It gave us peace of mind to give four pups to neighbors whose aging dogs would soon be gone to dog heaven. Pop assured me he had a foolproof plan for finding a dandy home for all of the remaining puppies. It wasn't long before he planned to haul a load of

culled cattle to the stockyards in Wichita. We loaded the pups in a big cardboard box and zoomed down Highway 54 toward the city. Enroute, Pop would pull off the highway and drive to the nearest farmstead, hoping to find a family with children. In such cases, Pop would take a puppy out of the box and place the soft, cuddly bundle of fur into the arms of a waiting child. In ninety percent of the cases, the excited boy or girl would convince the parents to let them keep the new furry friend. All six puppies were in new homes before we reached Wichita. Pop reassured me they would be happy with their new families and that satisfied my sense of remorse that they were gone.

Owning an array of dogs in my growing up years made those days much more fun and entertaining. It was amazing to me how forgiving a dog could be, even after being scolded for misbehaving. They were always cheerful and welcoming even after just a short time apart. Truly, dogs were a boy's best friend, adding greater joy and happiness to the life of a growing boy.

There is no such thing as a bad day
when you come home to a dog.

CHAPTER THIRTY-THREE

Exciting Adventures as a Page Boy

ை

The Kansas state capital city, Topeka, and the Kansas House of Representatives provided exciting times for me when I was eight through twelve years of age. My dad was elected to the Kansas Legislature as a member of the House of Representatives in 1927 and served admirably for a total of twenty-two years as a State Representative from the 93rd District, which included Kiowa County and those adjoining it. The Kansas House of Representatives and Senate met every other year, during even numbered years, with an occasional special session usually lasting a month or more if pressing legislation necessitated. Pop and Mama took Kenny and me with them to Topeka for the legislative sessions during the months of January through March. Once Kenny started high school, he stayed home during the sessions.

Pop took his responsibilities seriously and was a dedicated servant of his electorate, striving to enact laws that were honorable and beneficial to the average citizen.

Serving as a state representative required sincere dedication, close to volunteerism, due to the low pay that was allotted during the ninety-day session. Pop had a plaque hanging on the wall above his desk which stated, "A politician thinks of the next election, a statesman of the next generation." I often heard him say he preferred to think of

Marietta Weaver   Benjamin Weaver

himself as a down-to-earth man trying to avoid the trappings of politics.

Blallen had a lot of responsibility during those winter months while we were away. He handled the milking, fed the cattle, hogs, and chickens, and also cared for the newborn calves. He took pride in having the responsibility for the ranch and was intent upon doing his best to handle everything in the Mister's absence. He had been a cook in the Army so batching wasn't new or difficult for him.

Blallen subscribed to magazines of the day including *Holiday, Life,* and *Look*. He enjoyed those issues with vast numbers of pictures in each due to his inability to read. They almost told the story with pictures as he leafed through the pages. A six-volt, battery-powered radio crackled and hissed but did provide some news and entertainment for him through the winter months.

In early January, Pop, Mama, and I would load our belongings in the '31 Chevy and make the long, two hundred and fifty mile drive to Topeka. At least it seemed like a long way at forty miles per hour. Legislator's pay was three dollars per day and due to the low salary, my folks didn't feel they could afford to stay at the plush Jayhawk Hotel or Kansan Hotel frequented by wealthier legislators and lobbyists. Consequently, they searched for a furnished apartment in the *Topeka Daily Capital* classified ads. It was especially difficult to find housing within walking distance of the statehouse.

While reviewing available housing, I was instructed to remain in the Chevy since many apartment owners excluded children. At last an upstairs apartment was located and negotiations were proceeding with Mr. Bevans, the landlord. I was tired of waiting in the car at each stop and the folks were gone so long that I finally rang the door bell to join the group. Mr. Bevans exclaimed matter-of-factly, "I hope he isn't your little boy, because I don't rent to families with children and he's too big to take out and drown." Pop had a way with words and people. He assured Mr. Bevans they had "a fine son who obeyed his parents and was not destructive." He was quite persuasive and usually gained acceptance from the landlord. My bashful nature probably helped convince him.

January through March every other winter was really school a vacation for me. My grade school teachers were very cooperative and let me turn in my homework after returning to Mullinville in early April. They only required that I kept up with my classmates which posed no problem. Mama and Pop had been teachers and knew how to keep me on track with my lessons.

It was an exciting time for me to serve as a page boy in the huge Kansas House of Representatives where one hundred and twenty-five law makers were dealing with important matters and enacting legislation daily. We served as errand boys and messengers for the representatives by delivering messages, getting supplies from the Sergeant at Arms, bringing paperwork from their secretaries, and occasionally, running to the snack bar for treats.

Page boys received two dollars per day which gave me a wealthy feeling after getting an allowance of ten cents a week back home. We could run over to the Hi-way Diner across the street from the statehouse and eat our favorite meal of a hamburger, bowl of chili, and soda for twenty-five cents. The remaining dollar and seventy-five cents gave us plenty of spending money, especially when movies were only twenty-five cents.

As page boys, we had fun with our duties and even more excitement came when the house was adjourned. The House of Representatives often adjourned by three o'clock p.m. daily to allow time for various house committees to meet and debate the merits of the respective house bills emerging from the committees. Pages were only on duty when the House was in session so we had plenty of free time plus the run of the entire statehouse.

Payne Ratner was governor of Kansas during two legislative sessions. His son, Payne Jr., was a little older than I and was also a page. The opportunity to serve as a page made me feel mighty important. I was rubbing shoulders with sons of the governor and other important business or professional men serving as legislators. Tad and Todd Malone, twin sons of Representative Malone of Sedgwick County, a prominent Wichita attorney, were city kids and could think of more mischief than we naïve country bumpkins could ever imagine.

One of the Malone boys' favorite pranks was to take vortex or v-shaped paper cups from the large water cooler dispenser and then bend the rolled rim into fin shapes. When the finned paper cup full of water was dropped from the third story of the statehouse, it would twirl as it plunged to the ground floor, fifty feet below, splattering in all directions. It is amazing we were never caught in the act.

Another favorite pastime in the noon hour was to ride the freight elevator to the fifth floor of the statehouse. Then we would enter the stairway door leading to the statehouse dome and run up the seven hundred and ninety-five steps of criss-crossed steel stairway to the peak of the great structure. Darb Ratner, Governor Ratner's son, had a fancy combination wristwatch and stopwatch. He would clock our time for the trip up and down from the dome to see if we were gaining any speed from day to day.

Pop was known as the Poet Laureate of the House, reciting poetry as he noted special events. In addition, he levied various fines, such as a barrel of apples, on colleagues each time a suitable occasion arose. Mama was an active member of the Kansas Authors Club pursuing her writing projects during the session. On occasion, she was a ghost poetry writer for Pop and composed suitable renditions for each particular individual being fined. Most any occurrence qualified for a fine, ranging from a birthday, anniversary, a young legislator becoming engaged, getting married, or an older gentleman having a new grandchild. The legislator fined was billed for a barrel of ice cold, juicy Red Delicious apples. Fresh apples were a marvelous treat for us pages, especially since some of us were used to wormy, mealy windfall apples at home. One of our duties as pages was to deliver a shiny apple to each legislator's desk. Any representative who declined the offer brought a smile to our faces. That meant more for us.

My older sisters, Marjorie, Vivian, and Doris were attending Kansas State Teacher's College during those years and would usually visit us in Topeka sometime during the legislative session. On one such visit, Vivian brought along her boyfriend, Louis Bangs, a handsome six-foot two-inch tall college athlete to meet and, hopefully, impress Pop and Mama Weaver. She and Louis sat in the guest's gallery until the noon adjournment. Following lunch, I invited Big Lou to trek up to the statehouse dome with me. To my delight, he accepted the challenge. We hustled up the hundreds of steps, finally reaching the dome and the circular, railed viewing platform hundreds of feet above the statehouse grounds.

I suddenly discovered a big, Red Delicious apple crammed in my front pants pocket that was somewhat mashed from the trip and no longer edible. I didn't intend to mash it any longer and an idea popped into my mind. I exclaimed, "Big Lou, I'll bet you a nickel you can't throw this apple clear out to that statue on the statehouse lawn." I was really gambling big time.

Big Lou smiled broadly and without hesitation said, "It's a bet." He grasped my apple in his big hand, reared back in a pitching stance, and let it fly. We soon discovered how height and gravity affect a flying object. As the apple sailed through the air, it kept falling closer and closer to the base of the great capital building. It finally splattered on the sidewalk just a few steps ahead of a startled, dignified senator. He immediately looked upward, spied us, and then scurried on his way.

We didn't give the experience much thought except to be glad the apple hadn't conked the old gentleman on the head. As we were descending the stairway from the dome, we met two well-dressed men approaching us from the steps below. Before they said a word, I began to brag on how far Lou had thrown my apple from the dome. One man remarked, "Well, you two are just the guys we are looking for. Come with us!" I awkwardly looked at Big Lou, realizing my bragging had gotten us into big trouble.

We became more apprehensive when we eventually made it to the ground floor office with bold lettering on the door that read SERGEANT AT ARMS. I had no idea what that meant but it sounded scary. Big Lou looked none too happy either.

Once inside the office, a stern, uniformed officer began quizzing Lou as to what he was doing in the statehouse in the first place. Lou's only defense was that he was a guest of Representative Benjamin Weaver of Kiowa County. The grim interrogator looked doubtful. He stepped to the telephone and called the House to page for Representative Ben Weaver, requesting he report immediately to the Sergeant at Arms office. Things were looking worse; we were feeling much worse. Big Lou certainly had no intentions of impressing his girlfriend's father in this fashion.

A few nervous minutes ticked by before Pop entered the somber office, greeting us all cheerfully. This helped a bunch to relieve the tension in the air. The officer spoke in a firm voice and related the grave charges against us including "endangering the life of another human being" in his list of infractions. None of it seemed very dangerous to me.

Pop was a true diplomat and after an amiable visit with the officers he declared, "Louis is a fine young man, an outstanding college student, and had no intention of injuring anyone. I respectfully request you dismiss the charges." The officers talked among themselves, letting us squirm and sweat a few more minutes, before honoring the request to dismiss the charges. They admonished us to never again throw any object from the statehouse dome. We solemnly promised to honor their request.

It is probably an understatement that my sister, Vivian, was quite disturbed over the entire incident. Her desire to have Lou impress her parents had backfired. Fortunately, when things look darkest, there is always a silver lining. She and Louis were happily married two years later with our parents' blessing.

Another page buddy, Tim Booth of Wyandotte County, was a genius when it came to thinking of pranks to fill in our spare time during periods the House was not in session. One noon we trotted over to the big Kresge Five and Ten department store on Kansas Avenue where Tim spent ten cents on a large tube of copper BB's. He also recalled the joke, "What did the big cannon say to the smaller cannon?" We all looked mystified, so he remarked, "Let's get together and have some BB's!" We had a big laugh but still were baffled over his purchase since he had no BB gun.

Tim invited us to his parents' suite on the third floor of the Kansas Hotel. We followed him into their plush living quarters. He immediately raised the big window on the street side of the living room overlooking rows of parked cars below. Tim poured a few BB's in each of our palms and then proceeded to throw his handful out the window onto the hoods of the cars below. What a clatter they made. We could hardly wait to take our turns. By the time our BB supply was exhausted, pedestrians were scurrying and huddling together on the street below. They tried to dodge the errant orbs while anxiously looking upward. This alarmed Tim so he slammed the window and we high-tailed it back to the statehouse, unscathed.

It was common practice for the legislators to fire up their cigars, cigarettes, and pipes at will. Since Pop was staunchly opposed to alcohol and smoking, I had little exposure to either habit. It was intriguing for me to observe the smokers, especially those with pipes. My page position was on the front row of the House floor adjacent to the desk of Milt Poland from Doniphan County. Milt would ream the inside of his pipe bowl with a spoon-like device, unzip his leather tobacco pouch, then dip his pipe bowl into the tobacco, stopping occasionally to tamp it firmly during the process.

He had a round, silver pipe lighter that shot a flame directly into the packed bowl. I thought it was quite a handy device and much better than the kitchen matches used by Blallen back home. After a few cloudy puffs, he had his pipe all fired up and would lean back in the high-backed swivel desk chair to relax. The tobacco smoke had a fragrant aroma and he proudly informed me it was called Rum and

Maple. Milt seemed pleased I showed an interest and would occasionally tip me a whole dime for running special errands for him. Believe me, I was always ready for action even before he clapped his hands, a common signal to summon a page.

One evening I noticed a want-ad in the *Topeka Daily Capital* soliciting "ambitious boys to sell magazines and make extra spending money." This sounded too good to be true and I could hardly wait to report for an interview. The courteous magazine lady explained the plan to those of us who showed up and answered our questions. We were each furnished a canvas shoulder bag large enough to carry several magazines including *Colliers, Ladies Home Journal,* and *Redbook.* The names of the magazines were imprinted on the side of our bags, giving us free advertising. Each week we would report to the *Daily Capital,* return any unsold magazines, and receive our commission of fifteen cents for each one sold. We found that the legislators' secretaries and wives were our best customers.

A concession stand adjacent to the house chamber was operated by the Kansas School for the Blind. We could get a bottle of pop for a nickel there and soon made friends with Louie, a small, smiley man, who seemed to look forward to our visits. Louie was in charge of the stand and soon recognized each of us by our voices. Having never known a blind person, I was amazed with how he found his way around inside the stand. He loaded the iced pop coolers with different brands in set locations. In addition, he could identify each brand by bottle size and shape; likewise, he determined each coin denomination by feel. Louie impressed me so and became such a friend that I would occasionally write him in the spring after we returned to Eagle Canyon Ranch. His mother would read Louie the letters and then write me his friendly replies. I enjoyed his friendship and knowing Louie made me very thankful for sound eyesight.

For the session of 1940, I was thirteen and past the usual age for page boys, so I moved up to being a document room clerk which paid three dollars per day. What a pay increase. We were responsible for assembling the dozens of house bills that rolled off the printing press to be introduced by legislators each day.

We arranged stacks of one hundred and twenty-five pages per stack, in numerical order, around the perimeter of long tables. Then, in assembly line fashion, we followed each other around the tables, picking up one sheet of each bill until we had a complete set for each of the one hundred and twenty-five representatives. We wore soft rubber thumb and finger stalls on our thumbs and index fingers to facilitate grasping each sheet quickly. This assembly task needed little concentration so the older high school-age clerks were constantly chatting, telling tales and jokes as we worked. Most were unsuitable for us youngsters.

My freshman year at Mullinville Rural High School in the fall of 1940 brought a closure to winters spent in Topeka. In retrospect, I consider the legislative involvement as a highlight of my growing up years. Blallen endured those lonely, cold winter days and nights remarkably well with no one around but was always excited when we returned home and resumed normal activities. In later years, the family remained at the ranch while Pop served in the legislature.

Feeding cattle during the winter months was a daily task and I was big enough to do my share to help Blallen. Besides, I couldn't resist the offer to be hired as the school bus driver for our south route, a job my brother held the previous years while he was in high school. Best of all, it paid fifteen dollars per month.

To be hired as a school bus driver at age fourteen required something we rural kids had plenty of which was previous driving experience. The restricted chauffeur's license also required written and driving tests that were no problem. Living at the end of the bus route made it a natural for me. I could drop off all my twenty-one students along the bus route, park the bus at Eagle Canyon Ranch, then reverse the procedure the following morning. Pop let me park the big, yellow International school bus in the driveway of the red barn to ward off bad weather when snows arrived.

My job as bus driver included keeping the students safe and monitoring behavior. I took the job seriously since many of my passengers were grade school age. Once when one of the older boys was acting out, I stopped the bus along the side of the road and opened the side door. I walked back to where he was sitting and told him if he didn't straighten up, he could get out and walk. He gave me a sheepish look and nodded. I didn't have any trouble with anyone after that incident. Happily, I never had a bus accident or passenger injury during four years of high school. I felt mighty pleased.

The joy of living comes from
our encounters with new experiences.

CHAPTER THIRTY-FOUR

The Dangers of Tractor Driving

Since Blallen resisted driving a car, truck, or pick-up on the ranch, tractor driving was the favorite pastime for him. The boredom was broken up by the diversity of implements hitched to the tractor's draw bar. Springtime involved pulling a plowing, one-way, or tandem disk. The spring-tooth, field cultivator, and harrow prepared the seedbed for drilling wheat in the fall.

Blallen experienced an evolution of farm tractors as he bounced along on the spring steel seat, beginning with driving a 1932 John Deere on steel lugs. It jolted the tractor driver's bones as the lugs chewed into the hard, dry soil. In 1938, a new John Deere Model D tractor on rubber tires replaced the lugs. Bill felt he was in paradise with a smoother, cushioned ride.

There are plenty of precarious and risky tasks that must be done on a ranch. Not only do the livestock pose a danger anytime they are tended, but farm machinery is plenty hazardous. Operating a tractor is one task that has its risks. Old timers were beginning to notice that the constant roar of threshing machines, tractors, and other motorized equipment gradually affected their hearing. Similarly, working in the dust of a harvest field, putting up hay, or cultivating crop land took its toll on the lungs. Even the daily operation of a tractor could turn deadly in a flash. In the thousands of miles Blallen

drove, he only experienced two serious accidents, either of which could have been fatal.

One sunny day as Blallen was bouncing along on the steel lug tractor, the rear wheel suddenly dropped off into an eighteen-inch sinkhole. The violent, sudden lurch of the tractor threw Blallen off the spring seat onto the dirt and directly in front of the wheat drill he was pulling. The tractor climbed out of the sink hole and continued forward as Blallen hit the ground. He frantically began scooting and rolling to get clear of the drill. Unfortunately, the steel drill passed over his barrel-shaped chest. In doing so, the wheel raised the sharp discs high enough to prevent slashing his legs. The heavy drill, loaded with wheat, crushed all the air out of Blallen's lungs, leaving him gasping for breath. Fortunately, the Mister was nearby mending a barbed wire fence and spotted the tractor chugging along without a driver. Pop rushed to Blallen's aid and managed to get him into the old pick-up and then sped toward Mullinville to Doc Puckett's office. After an examination, Doc pronounced Blallen had two broken ribs. He was lucky to be alive. Wide bands of heavy cloth encompassed his upper body and were to remain in place for several days before Blallen could return to tractor driving.

Three or four years later, Blallen was driving the tractor pulling a binder which was powered by a power takeoff (PTO) on the tractor. The whirling, exposed universal joint drive should always be covered with a metal shield to protect the operator from injury. For some reason, the shield was missing and Blallen got one leg close enough to the PTO for it to grab a hold of one pant leg on his baggy overalls. The force of the PTO began tightening and yanking and ripped his worn overalls completely off, leaving Blallen in his B.V.Ds. The ragged, weakened denim material in his well-worn overalls saved Blallen. He could have been badly maimed or killed had he been whipped around the powerful shaft. Considering his more than thirty years of operating a tractor, Blallen was most fortunate that he only had two near-miss accidents.

Better a thousand times careful than once dead.

CHAPTER THIRTY-FIVE

How Not to Move a Pool Table

One place that my brother, Kenny, and I were not permitted to frequent in town was Hock Aldrich's Pool Hall, east of Nolan's Garage, primarily because the loafers and pool players were smoking and betting money on the pool games. Pop was the oldest son of a Methodist preacher and took a hard stand against smoking, chewing, swearing, drinking, and gambling. Unbeknownst to Pop, or so we thought, was that Hock's daughter, Ramona, was sweet on Kenny and she constantly asked why he couldn't come to the pool hall. Kenny was well aware that in our little town he would never keep it a secret from our parents if he ever tried to sneak a visit to the pool hall.

Led on by my big brother, the two of us often moaned and lamented about not being allowed to learn to play pool. We couldn't see any harm in mastering a challenging game that required such skill, accuracy, and strategy. Little did we know that Pop had planned to buy a pool table when the pool hall closed and put the tables up for sale. It was an exciting day when the auctioneer

yelled "sold" to Pop's bargain-priced bid. Now we were the proud owners of a gigantic, solid wood pool table, complete with a six-inch slate table-bed.

The next big challenge was to move the table from the pool hall, across the railroad tracks, pull the load nine miles to our ranch, and slowly tow the monstrosity down the steep, sloping driveway to the ranch house. As we made plans and prepared to haul the pool table to the ranch, we quickly learned the heavy slate slabs made the table weigh a half-ton or more. Pop lined up eight men to be at the pool hall to help us load the table into our old stock trailer, pulled by our 1930s ranch truck. After groaning, straining, and maneuvering the table into the rattle-trap stock trailer, the men sent us off to the ranch with gasps of relief and a rather ominous chorus of "Good luck!" Pop seemed quite confident and thought nothing of the heavy load after years of hauling two thousand pound Marriage Mulley bulls to various buyers.

Pop decided that the old bunk room and former orphan boy's dormitory room at the ranch house was an ideal spot for a pool table since the room had a solid concrete floor and could support the weight. The big obstacle was how to get the pool table down one story and into the room. The enclosed stairway between the bunk room and the house was too narrow, leaving only the west door as a possible entryway for the table. However, the only access to the doorway was from a canyon bank that had washed out and worn

Driveway to House   Bunkroom Door

away over the years after the room was built. This left a twenty-foot drop from the top of the door to the canyon floor below the room. Blallen, our ever-faithful hired man, suggested he could set up a gin pole in the canyon bank west of the bunk room and hang a heavy block and tackle at the gin top. Then he could tie a rope around the table hitched to the block and tackle and ease the bulky load down through the open door.

Another heavy rope was secured around the girth of the table and also hitched to the gin top as a safety measure in case something broke loose. We thought he was a genius! Once our plan was underway, we pushed, shoved, and pulled and eventually had the pool table out of the trailer and suspended in mid-air near the bunk room doorway. Blallen's idea to use a back-up rope turned out to be a wise move since the old, dry sisal rope that was strung through the blocks snapped and broke about the time the table was half-way down the side of the building.

There we were with our enormous wooden pool table dangling like a wrecker ball in mid-air. The much anticipated pool table hung there day after day, like waiting for Christmas, until the lumber yard in town could order enough footage of heavy rope to re-string the block and tackle. Pop was always praying for rain but this was one time we hoped the rain could wait until our pool table was delivered to its proper place inside the bunk room. Kenny and I could barely contain ourselves, never having believed that "anticipation is half the pleasure of receiving." We all had our fingers crossed that the spare rope tied around the table would hold the dead weight of a thousand pounds until help arrived.

Finally, the telephone rang and Culley's Hardware informed us the new rope had arrived. On our next trip to town, we retrieved the special delivery. Blallen was able to re-string the blocks with new rope and the table moving and installation project was re-started. It required some barnyard engineering to figure out how to maneuver the heavy, bulky load into the center of the room where it would come to rest as we lowered it through the doorway. Eventually, we eased the table down on end through the open door and to its final resting place.

Wow! Were we in tall cotton having our own recreation room and a place to spend hours perfecting our shots while playing hundreds of pool games! It was a great way to pass the time on rainy days or after a long day of ranch chores. The forbidden pleasure was finally ours and we couldn't wait to have our buddies come to the ranch and share in our excitement and fun.

What we wait for is not as important as
what we learn from waiting.

CHAPTER THIRTY-SIX

Globe Trotters in Mullinville

The high school fall semester of 1938 was underway when Principal Roger Arnold learned that the famous Harlem Globe Trotters would be touring the Midwest. Since Arnold was also the basketball coach, this news spurred him to thinking how exciting it would be to have them stop in Mullinville for a performance on their route to Denver. He conferred with School Board President Ben Weaver about that possibility. Both were favorable and presented the proposition to the school board which voted unanimous approval to sponsor the game, feeling confident there would be a sell-out of spectator tickets. It would be a once-in-a-lifetime event to have such a renowned team appear in our little town.

Excitement filled the air in the Mullinville community and surrounding areas when news spread that the Harlem Globe Trotters would soon be playing basketball at the Mullinville Rural High School gymnasium. Listening to their famous basketball performances on the radio thrilled sports fans far and wide, further elevating expectations. Widespread

advertising reached all over the map resulting in a sellout of the ground floor gymnasium plus an overflowing balcony packed with excited spectators.

At seven o'clock p.m., the high school pep band played two rousing marches as the greatly anticipated moment arrived. A tall, lanky Globe Trotter dashed onto the court from the south door of the gymnasium, spinning a basketball on the index finger of each hand. What a deafening roar arose from the crowd as Duke Chamberlain sped down the court. He was speedily followed by Sonny Boswell dribbling a basketball between his legs as he raced down the court. The other three Trotters dashed in and ran in a figure-eight as they passed the basketball behind their backs at full speed. As the crowd cheered and clapped, the din was tremendous. The Mullinville Town Team, who were really great sports to oppose such a renowned team, then sped onto the court passing back and forth

Coach Arnold served as the referee. He called the teams to the center court circle for a jump ball to start the game. He gave a sharp blast on his official whistle. Just as he prepared to throw the ball upward, Zack Clayton dropped on his hands and knees behind Coach Arnold. Their center was six-feet-three-inch Inman "Big Jack" Jackson who had a flair for showboating. Big Jack pushed Coach over backward and a third player caught Coach Arnold before he hit the gym floor. The crowd roared as Coach, somewhat shaken, took it in good stead. A second attempted jump ball was completed.

Such dribbling, passing, and constant shouting by Duke to team members kept the crown in an uproar. A favorite antic by Zack Clayton was to palm the basketball in his huge hand, then fake passing it while gripping the ball tightly. Then he dribbled and made a bounce pass to another team member who promptly swished the net with a dead-eye shot. During the exciting game, Duke kept up his line of chatter, yelling to his teammates as they passed and dribbled down the court. One Trotter could dribble the ball only two or three inches from the court floor, then gradually increase the height as he moved along. One of the most impressive moves was when Boswell got fouled. He would throw his free throw from the opponent's free throw line and amazingly, would sink it. Boswell was well-known for making long distance trick shots.

During a time out, Clayton grabbed a water bucket and threw the contents into the crowd. All expected a water bath, but it turned out to be confetti. Pandemonium reigned. The alert high school janitors quickly grabbed their wide mops to clear away the slippery debris.

Every spectator seemed to have a hilarious time enjoying the game which involved wild passing, phenomenal dribbling, amazing trick shots, and leaps that were higher than the basket rim. The courageous town team members played their best, but were no match for the height of the professional ball handlers.

Following the great game, Pop and Roger accompanied the Trotters and their tour bus to the coffee shop in Mullinville for a Kansas steak dinner. Once the team filed into the coffee shop the cook exclaimed, "I don't feed no n****** in my establishment." Pop and Roger were mortified, embarrassed, and disgusted at such a retort. They turned on their heels, loaded the bus, and drove to Greensburg for a delicious steak dinner. In retrospect, the 1930s were difficult times for African-Americans as discrimination and racism were rampant. But, the Harlem Globe Trotters were undaunted and expressed their appreciation for being invited to a small, but lively town in southwest Kansas.

Appreciate that life is made up of moments.

CHAPTER THIRTY-SEVEN

Halloween Pranks

Many small towns in southwest Kansas endured unusual antics each Halloween. The pranks were instigated by high school students or recent graduates who spent the entire year thinking of shenanigans they could try when the big day arrived. Many of them compared ideas with friends or family members in other small towns around the area. There was never a lack of wild stunts to pull, just a lack of help to pull off the plans. It seemed that each year the troublemakers were trying to outdo the antics of the previous year. The local marshals always seemed to be at the wrong end of town as the action was taking place.

HALLOWEEN JOLLITY WITHIN REASON NEED

Parents Urged to Curb Wild Pranks of Youngsters.

Blocking off Main Street was a common goal to let local residents know there had been plenty of tomfoolery going on during the night. Materials most often used to barricade the main street of town were confiscated from the local lumberyard. Somehow the six-foot chain link fence around the lumberyard was no obstacle for pranksters. Large livestock water tanks were rolled onto Main Street, soon followed by hundreds of fence posts, rolls of woven wire, and piles of lumber to form a giant blockade across the entire street. It became a mountain of materials ready to greet morning traffic. While most of the pranks were in fun and not intended to cause malicious damage or destruction of property, the time and effort to clean up the mess from the previous night somehow took most of the following day.

Those not involved in the blockade were busy pushing over rickety outhouses that were not well anchored. That prank resulted in a strong odor emerging from the open pit where the outhouse once stood. Occasionally, ardent outhouse pushers gave one too many lunges in their efforts to up-end the old privies. This resulted in the pranksters losing their balance and landing in the terrible pit of sewage below the outhouse, an experience never forgotten.

One group of serious pranksters created quite a disturbance by relocating a neighbor's grain hauling wagon. First, they dismantled the wagon by removing all four heavy wagon wheels which was a large task in itself. The wagon bed was carried by a dozen strong backs up the steel fire escape stairway to the top of the Mullinville City Building. Then, wheels followed and were reassembled to the wagon bed. The following morning, an entire grain wagon greeted citizens from the rooftop. This was a popular annual prank since everyone in town doing business the next day at the City Building would be greeted by the wagon. The marshal took plenty of joking and ridicule about not being able to catch the pranksters in the act year after year.

HALLOWEEN PRANKS NIPPED IN BUD BY STRONG ARM OF LAW

One of the more creative escapades occurred in the mid-1930s. The janitor, principal, and teachers at Mullinville High School arrived to work early the morning after Halloween to find a large cow on top of the high school. She was bawling, mooing and creating quite a ruckus. No one could figure out how in the world that cow got up there, but it was obvious that leading a cow down a stairway was not going to happen. The high school students were agog with the situation and could hardly keep their minds on their classes wondering who among the student body could have been involved. The principal and teachers did their best to stifle all the rumoring and gossiping about the incident, hoping to show their severe disapproval and prevent the prank from being repeated the following year. It disrupted the entire day at school which was obviously the intention of the mischief-makers. Not only did it require a gin pole and a huge sling to lower the cow to the ground, but there was a terrible mess of manure to clean up and remove from the rooftop. It was never determined who was involved but it was highly suspicious. My sister, Doris, always had a huge smile on her face when the prank was mentioned, as if she knew something about who was involved. Being of high school age and the daughter of the school board president, she seemed to be clued-in to the mischief.

After years of more incidents and escalating creativity on the part of the tricksters, Neil Fralle, a local bachelor and farmer, decided it was time to put a stop to such nonsense. Since the local marshal seemed to have no control, Neil vowed and bragged that he would end the annual disturbances. Word got around that Neil was a force to be reckoned with and the local trouble-makers were put on notice. The following Halloween, Neil arrived in town at sundown and began slowly cruising up and down Main Street in his old pickup. Two hours went by and there was little happening. Neil was surely chuckling to himself about how easy it was to be in control "if you just know how to handle such situations."

As Neil drove into his driveway at daybreak the next morning, he was applauding himself for having successfully stifled the annual Halloween ordeal in Mullinville. Unbeknownst to Neil, the usual pranksters were paying a visit to his farmhouse south of town while he dutifully spent the night patrolling in town. A gentle milk cow was led into his kitchen accompanied by a dozen fat hens turned loose in the living room. As he opened his kitchen door, a fat hen squawked and flew past his ear as feathers flew. Neil was then greeted by the mooing of old Buttercup, his only milk cow. Needless to say, Neil never volunteered for patrol again.

Pranks can be fun if no damage is done or
if it's happening to somebody else.

CHAPTER THIRTY-EIGHT

High School Days and Beyond

Enrolling at Mullinville Rural High School in the fall of 1941 was an exciting transition from grade school. All twenty-two of our class members graduated together from the eighth grade. My folks gave me my first wristwatch with a spring-steel wristband as an eighth grade graduation gift. I was proud as punch especially since few kids had wristwatches and the fact that it cost twelve dollars and fifty cents when money was scarce. I treated that watch as if it were priceless, only wearing it to church or on special occasions to keep it from getting filled with dust or the crystal broken.

The first beneficial situation upon starting high school was an offer from the school district to drive a twenty-four passenger school bus during the school year. In those days it was impossible to find men who could drive the bus on a rural route in the mornings and afternoons, work part-time somewhere else, and make enough to support a family.

Having grown up driving cars, pickups, and tractors, the job of being a school bus driver was most appealing to me. We lived the farthest distance from town along

one of the four rural bus routes which gave me the advantage of picking up neighboring students along the route to town and then letting them off on the way home after school. I could then park the school bus in a barn stall at the ranch ready for the next day's run. Another great incentive was being paid fifteen dollars a month. That really served as a clincher to accept the offer at a time when a dollar had much buying power. During winter when snow made our dirt roads into a slick and muddy quagmire, it was truly a challenge. I was most grateful that I had kindly, well-behaved school children as passengers and no accidents of any kind during the four years I drove the bus.

My four years at Mullinville Rural High School were filled with activities and excitement. Although studies came first, extra-curricular activities were the fun times. The mood in our community was beginning to improve as the terrible drought of the 1930s had broken when normal rains returned in 1939 and farmers were getting back on their feet. The optimism was dampened by the worries about the war in Europe but even that created more demand for farm commodities. Summers were filled with hard work on the ranch and I looked forward to the school term to have good times with my friends.

During grade school I was in the band and played the handed-down clarinet that Doris played in high school. My mother played the clarinet years before and must have encouraged it. Now that I was a high school freshman, the clarinet seemed much too sissified to me. Fortunately, our music director, Mr. Victor Klassen, saved me from dropping out of band by offering to let me play one of the two school sousaphones. I was elated and played that giant-belled instrument all through high school. Mr. Klassen had me singing in the boys chorus as well as the mixed chorus, all of which added to the pleasure of high school days. I sang bass so learning the bass clef on the sousaphone while singing bass in choir came in mighty handy. Our music department put on band concerts and vocal performances all during the school year, giving us the fun of performing before proud parents.

Woodshop was always exciting with Mr. Chandler as our instructor. He was rather stern and disciplined. Absolutely no candy eating or gum chewing was allowed during shop class. Of course, it was tempting to try to violate his rigid rule. Our punishment was to have our candy or gum confiscated and then he would sit at his desk and enjoy the prize. This was very upsetting to Karl Burnett who had spent a whole nickel on a package of peppermint Chiclets. It was murder to watch Mr. Chandler consume them.

The following week, Karl brought another package of Chiclets to shop class except the shiny package was filled with Feen-a-mint, a powerful laxative. Karl let himself get caught chewing and, of course,  Mr. Chandler confiscated his gum and began chewing it himself. Our shop class was the first period of the day. Later classes reported that Mr. Chandler spent much of his time in the boy's restroom during the later shop periods that day. Karl had achieved his revenge although the Feen-a-mint cost him fifteen cents more than Chiclets.

Sports were attractive, especially in the spring when Coach Wilde organized a school baseball team. There had been a Mullinville town baseball team for years but team members were men who had already finished school. I was fortunate to be assigned to first base and legally could use a sock-type first base glove, giving me greater security in snagging a ball thrown from the infield to put a runner out on first base. We traveled to various towns in our league to play baseball games and competed in tournaments with many fun experiences.

Our Mullinville Tigers basketball team was most exciting for me. Kenny had been an excellent player during his high school years and even had a basketball goal put up at the ranch so he could practice. I was impressed with the trophies won by the teams of his era. It meant a lot to me to be part of another winning team at MRHS.

Miss Crawford, our English literature teacher, was the dramatics coach and directed a class play each semester. Much joking and laughter went on during play practices as we enjoyed a break from classroom subjects or study hall. Our senior class play was a murder mystery. Myron McKinley stole the show as a bungling sheriff named Jackson who was heading the murder investigation. For months afterward, Myron carried the nickname Jackson. He also was chosen to drive the school bus route north of Mullinville. He had the distinction of being assigned the only wooden-bodied school bus which was a 1920s model from the original fleet of Mullinville school buses. The only steel parts were the hood, engine, and fenders. That old bus was loose in every window, door, and joint and earned the name of "The Rattle-Trap." Myron was a real sport and drove "Old Shaky" all four years of high school.

While our senior year was advancing in early 1945, World War Two was still raging and the draft was in full effect, enlisting every able-bodied young man age eighteen or older. My brother had already joined the Army Air Corps in 1942 and many other boys from our little town were serving in other branches of the military. A few guys in our class decided we would prefer joining the Navy rather than becoming what Blallen called "cannon-fodder" in the Army. Six of us enlisted in the Navy in early 1945 to report for duty on May 22, 1945, a week after high school graduation. Being seventeen, we had our parent's signed consent and reported to a Kansas City recruitment station where we boarded a troop train headed for San Diego. Many of us had never been away from home more than a few days in our lives. Somehow the momentous completion of high school was overshadowed by the need to grow up quickly and serve our country. Pop had been president of the school board since 1919 and with my graduation, had the pleasure and honor of handing a graduation diploma to all of his five children while serving as president of the board. He eventually served forty-five years in that position and joked about knowing how Moses must have felt.

Boot camp at the Naval Training Center was a rigorous experience. Upon arrival, our hair was shortened almost to our scalps and we were given multiple shots and vaccinations, making it painful to raise either arm. Chief Nitzel forewarned that we boots would be toughened up during our daily calisthenics on what he called the grinder, an asphalt pad as large as a football field. The June San Diego sun beating down on the grinder made it hot to the touch when doing pushups, a favorite torment of our merciless platoon leader.

Our entire Company #367 moaned, groaned, and ached during the boot camp ordeal. We farm-oriented boys had done manual labor in full sun which made the experience a little more bearable. I did feel sorry for the city boots who had flabby muscles and had not been exposed to sunshine. Even their heads peeled due to the intense sun on the grinder.

Nearly all our company, except a few drop-outs who were sent home on medical discharges, survived boot camp and we were sent to a deployment center, Camp Roberts, east of San Francisco. While we waited to be assigned to a ship, the war ended. It seemed the Navy didn't know what to do with us. We were lying on a hard bunk in the barracks for hours doing nothing. It was a truly boring experience.

One day a Chief came into the barracks and shouted, "Can any of you swabbies run a typewriter?" Three of us sounded off, defying all advice to never volunteer for anything in the Navy. We packed our sea bags and were soon shipped to the Naval Air Base at Norman, Oklahoma. Somehow it seemed like a good idea to be stationed closer to home. There we spent our remaining Navy days typing out discharge papers for Navy veterans returning from various theaters of operation.

May 22, 1946 was the date scheduled to close the Norman Naval base. We typed out our own discharge papers, had them signed by the base commander, grabbed our sea bags, and boarded buses homeward bound, a joyous day for each of us. None of our Company felt like heroes although we had the satisfaction of knowing we were prepared to be assigned to a ship and active war duty if needed.

A world of opportunities, just for the asking.

CHAPTER THIRTY-NINE

Mullinville Tigers Basketball Team

Our small town of Mullinville in southwest Kansas had a long history of strong basketball teams. Despite being a small school with fewer than twenty students in each high school class, the Fighting Tigers of Mullinville Rural High School often defeated teams from larger towns with schools of much higher enrollment.

One special season to be remembered was that of 1944-45 near the end of World War Two. Starting team members included three Seniors and two Juniors. They were Dorl Rader, #33, at guard; Lyle Rader #22 at forward; Glenn Headrick, #44 at forward; Max Liggett, #66 at forward, and Eldon Weaver, #55 at center. Dorl and Lyle were brothers, one class apart in high school, and sons of Dillie Rader, who was a star basketball player of a generation previous.

Dorl's deadliest shot was a push-off from his extended left palm. Lyle used an accurate two-handed shot from behind his head which was very difficult for defenders to guard. Glenn had a very accurate two-handed push shot as well. Eldon was the team's top rebounder and handled the jump ball duties. Curtis Tarrant and Bob Aldrich were the only other players on the team who could be substituted if one of the starting five fouled out of the game.

The team's dedicated coach, W. O. Shelby, inspired us to play harder in our efforts to qualify for the state tournament. We didn't think of ourselves as particularly talented basketball players and certainly didn't have the advantages of height on our side. Glenn was our shortest player at five-feet-seven inches, Dorl was five-feet-eight, Lyle was five-feet-nine, Max was five-feet-ten, and Eldon was tallest at six feet. Regardless of size, we were hard-working farm boys who knew the importance of giving it our all and working together against the odds to get a tough job done. It seemed that the war effort of the past four years gave us additional incentive to be willing to fight and win. Most of all, we wanted to do our best in representing our town and school and give them pride in our efforts.

We attributed much of our success to our many loyal fans and spectators whose wild cheering and encouraging shouts spurred us on to play even harder. Such excited, boisterous support gave us added momentum and inspiration to win. Our energetic cheerleading squad, led by Martha Sidener, filled the gymnasium with rousing outbursts. "Hit 'em high, hit 'em low. C'mon Tigers, let's go!" resonated across the court and filled the gym. The sounds of the pep band brought the crowd to its feet when Bill Campbell on trumpet electrified the crowd with his brilliant fanfares. Along with Eloise Fralick on saxophone and Faye Sloan on baritone, the band belted out resounding, melodious tunes to support our team.

At every Mullinville home game, the gymnasium was packed on both the ground floor and in the suspended wooden balcony. The Fighting Tigers fired up the crowd prior to each game by passing the ball back and forth as we raced down the length of the court in a figure-eight formation. We imagined ourselves like the Harlem Globe

Trotters who had performed in this very same gymnasium in Mullinville years earlier. The throng of fans cheered and stomped their feet on the balcony floor creating a drum-like resonation inside the packed gymnasium. Our opponents trembled. The showy figure-eight

drill ended when the referee's piercing whistle signaled us to start the contest and assemble for the jump ball at the center court.

Eldon was the tallest player on the team and usually "got the tip," giving the Tigers the ball and a good chance of sinking the first basket and putting the first two points on the scoreboard. Our exciting fast break won many games for us. Dorl, Lyle, and Glenn were skillful ball handlers and led the charge. We sped down the court as rapidly as possible hoping to get within shooting range before the opponent could set up their zone or man-to-man defense.

We had a highly successful season and earned our way to the Regional tournament at Garden City. The Tigers won twenty-two straight games, then went on to win the Regional tournament at Garden City with a record of twenty-five wins and no losses, thus qualifying for the Kansas State Basketball Tournament at Hutchinson in the spring of 1945. Excitement reigned as we traveled to Hutchinson to take on Attica in the Class B bracket of the tournament. Big cities such as Wyandotte, Wichita, or Topeka with enrollment of four hundred and seventy-five or more competed in Class AA, medium sized towns such as Hays, Augusta, or Wellington, with enrollments of less than four hundred and seventy-five competed in Class A, and small towns with enrollments of less than one hundred and fifty competed in Class B. Our tournament featured sixteen teams from small towns such as Kipp, Palco, Courtland, Lorraine, Strawn, Halstead, and Pretty Prairie.

We were both thrilled and nervous at the prospect of competing in the much larger gymnasium at Hutchinson. It was half again as large as our gym and we were awed by the distances and difficulty in getting our bearings in the spacious sports arena. Like many other teams, the idea of being in a much larger city, away from home, and in unfamiliar surroundings made it difficult to contain our excitement. For some of our team members, the trip to the basketball tournament was the first night we had ever been away from home on our own without our parents. Mr. Rader was one of our biggest fans and accompanied the team to all our games.

As expected, our basketball trips gave us many memorable experiences. One of our boyish escapades was the night of the pillow fight in our hotel room just before lights out. Pillows were flying and blows were landing until all of a sudden, one of the pillows missed the target, sailed out the open window, and landed on the sidewalk outside the hotel. We all glanced at each other like a boy caught with his hand in the cookie jar. Then, we goaded the guilty team member into retrieving the pillow he had thrown out the window. He was further shamed into action because he was the one who started the pillow fight. Our second floor hotel room was equipped with a heavy rope to be used in case of fire, so we persuaded him to shinny down the rope and retrieve the pillow. Once on the ground, one of the other boys pulled up the rope, leaving the fellow stranded on the sidewalk wearing only his shorts, a definite no-no. He begged and pleaded for us to throw him the rope before someone saw him, but he was told it was all his fault and he had to come back to the room through the hotel lobby. After a good laugh among us in the hotel room, we lowered the rope and helped our distraught teammate back through the window.

We had never seen parking meters until our trip to Hutchinson. We made a game of leap-frogging over the parking meters as we walked down the street to the cafe. Our antics ended when one of our players didn't leap quite high enough and came crashing down after a failed attempt to leap over a meter.

Our first opponent in the state tournament was Attica. We gave it our all as we pressured them and pushed ourselves to make our fast break work to our advantage on the huge court. It was a struggle to get our bearings and we were well below our normal field goal completion percentage. Having been accustomed to a two-thirds size court, many of our shots fell short of the hoop. The final score was 46-27 as Attica advanced to take on Halstead, state champions of the previous year, who soundly beat Attica 51-21. Halstead went on to win the tournament beating Pretty Prairie 44-30. We were disappointed with our loss but thrilled to have the experience at the state tournament. Our nerves and the unfamiliar court were our demise despite giving our best effort. We had such high hopes of bringing home a state title to our parents, fans, and hometown residents. Despite our loss, Mullinville welcomed us home and celebrated our final record of 25 wins-1 loss for the 1944-45 season. Thrills and triumphs of that memorable year were not to be defined by that final game.

You aren't defeated unless you quit.

Mullinville First Team with Trophies 1944-45
Lyle Rader-22, Max Liggett-66, Eldon Weaver-55, Dorl Rader-33,
Glenn Headrick-44
First Place in Invitational Tournament at Coates
First Place in District Tournament at Ford
First Place in Regional Tournament at Garden City

Appendix

I. Bill Allen - The rest of the story

After a difficult home life as a child, being part of a caring family was a welcome experience for Blallen. No one would have imagined the drifter hired hand would stay on and live at Eagle Canyon Ranch until he retired. He didn't talk much about himself or his family but Mama eventually learned that Blallen was two years older than she, making him about forty-five years old when he first arrived at the ranch. No wonder he seemed old to all of us kids.

Blallen earned a fair wage at the time of one dollar a day plus his room and board at the ranch house with the family. His first year's wages came to two hundred ninety-one dollars plus sixty-seven dollars in interest. Plenty of food, a comfortable home, and companionship gave him great security and pleasure. Blallen didn't seem too concerned about money and was happy to be paid once a year for his wages plus interest. Mama helped him keep track of his accounts and look after his check book. Only one time was he bamboozled out of money. A shifty magazine salesman conned Blallen when he took Blallen's seven dollar check to the bank and forged it as seventy dollars. It upset Mama more than Blallen that the bank cashier wasn't more suspicious, knowing Blallen couldn't read and only looked at the magazine pictures. "How could a man need that many magazines?" Mama wondered.

Pop and Mama were always troubled that Blallen was at severe odds with his brother, Arthur. They hadn't spoken or contacted each other for more than thirty years. The falling out stemmed from what Blallen thought was an unfair inheritance of their father's small Nebraska farm in which Arthur was the primary benefactor. Much searching, calling, and writing helped the Weavers locate Arthur and his wife in Orchard, Nebraska. Relatives meant so much to the Weaver families that they were determined to get Blallen and Arthur reconciled, although it took strong coercion and a trip to Nebraska to finally bring them together. Their reward was to see two brothers once again re-united and at peace with each other. Mama finally came to learn that Blallen had a brother, Oscar, who lived at Colby, Kansas and another brother, Fred, in Nebraska.

The ultimate experience in tractor driving for Blallen was in 1951, a rare bumper wheat crop year, when a used 1949 John Deere R  diesel on rubber tires was purchased. The ride was not only improved, but the power and ground speed nearly doubled over the previous models. Blallen felt like the king-of-the-mountain when he drove the larger machine complete with a vinyl covered cushioned seat. He probably spent the equivalent of four years driving a tractor during his time at the ranch and no telling how many thousands of miles he drove.

Calculating the number of gallons of milk Blallen carried from the big barn down the hill to the ranch house, twice a day for all those years, Blallen would have filled three stainless steel milk tankers of five thousand gallons each during his time at the ranch. Why wasn't the milk separator at the barn? Simply because it was easier to clean the separator with hot, soapy water by having it at the house.

Years later, Blallen continued the shopping trip tradition with the Weaver grandchildren when the families came to visit during the summer or at Christmas. Blallen was especially fond of all thirteen of the grandchildren, almost as if they were kinfolk related to him. He doted on them when they were at the ranch. They were always in need of new clothes, shoes, or toys.

The Mister (Pop Weaver) and Blallen

Although he never wore cowboy boots, buying each grandson a pair of boots at age five or six pleased him a great deal. The granddaughters were outfitted in a new dress or fancy shoes chosen by their mothers and much to their delight.

Blallen, in his three decades on the ranch as a family member, shared the joy of seeing the three Weaver girls graduate from college and later attended two of their weddings held in the ranch house parlor. Blallen was on hand when Kenneth enlisted in the Air Force in 1942 and when Eldon enlisted in the Navy in 1945. As a combat veteran, Blallen knew the potential risks and difficulties the boys might face during wartime. Later, he was part of the family Christmas celebrations and homecomings as the Weaver Five brought their families back to the ranch. He looked forward to the family events as much or more than anyone.

After years of banking his wages with little expenditure, Blallen had accumulated a sizeable bank account. Mama periodically would have him transfer his funds from a checking account to a savings account or purchase U.S. Savings Bonds paying good interest rates.

As he grew older, he pondered what to do with his estate. Mama knew how he doted over the children of the Weaver Five whom he watched grow up on Eagle Canyon Ranch. He seemed to think of their families as his own and Mama suggested he might like to give each one a U.S. Savings Bond as a gift. Deciding on what denomination of bond to give was his next consideration. After detailed calculations, giving each of the thirteen grandchildren a five hundred dollar savings bond would still leave him plenty of funds for retirement. What a generous and unexpected gift for each grateful recipient! One grandchild, D'Lee, exclaimed, "I'm an heiress!"

The Eldon Weaver family lived on the ranch for several years and Eldon's four children, known as the Four T's, were more closely involved with Blallen. Blallen watched the toddlers grow up and learn to call him Blallen or Sandy-man. He loved to hold them on his knee and it most likely gave him a feeling of having grandchildren of his own. Blallen was especially fond of Trudy and wanted to hold her

when he stopped by the Weaver house for a visit on the way to or from the fields and the ranch house. It was quite a sight to see a little two-year-old girl sitting in the lap of an unshaven, sixty-five-year-old ranch hand. Fortunately, his grease and tobacco stained bib overalls never seemed to rub off on her clean dresses.

Out of scrap lumber and used tin sheets, Blallen constructed a one room playhouse for the Four T's, complete with a front door and windows on each side. When the family moved to Kiowa in 1957, Blallen and Pop managed to load the playhouse on a farm truck and haul it to Kiowa. They set it on cement blocks in the back yard

under the huge mulberry tree. The Four T's spent hours playing in the playhouse and eventually it became part of an obstacle course they created for climbing from the tree to the top of the playhouse and down a branch to the ground.

As Blallen grew older, he found it difficult to live on his own and the years of working in dusty situations had taken a toll on his lungs. Ben and Marietta felt he certainly had earned the rights as a veteran of World War I to be admitted to a Veteran's Administration facility for his retirement years. Blallen kept few records which made it difficult to provide proof of his military service. Blallen served in the 85th Division, 355 Regiment, 163rd Depot Brigade. By much persistence at the state level and with assistance from the American Legion, they were able to get him admitted to the Fort Dodge Kansas Veteran's Home. He passed away in 1960 at age 73 and was buried in Orchard, Nebraska near his parents, John and Kate.

II. City Cousins Grow Up

It seemed to Pop and Mama that the city cousins might never grow up and make something of themselves. Sometimes Pop thought the boys "didn't have enough sense to pound sand into a rat hole." Other times when he was totally exasperated with a boy, Pop would say, "he just isn't worth shooting."

The City Cousins' ranch reunions ended as the boys became teenagers and thought they were too old to come to the ranch to work. But the summers of work and responsibility taught the boys a few lessons. They each went on to create their own accomplishments.

Ernie "Hogwallow" Reiger completed medical school at Kansas University and spent one study year in Sweden where he met Karin. They were married and he brought her back home as his bride. Ernie became a surgeon and practiced medicine for twenty-five years at Wesley Medical Center in Wichita. Upon retirement, he and Karin operated Reiger Medical Supply in Wichita.

Bobby Reiger was a natural at sales and marketing. He specialized in contracting to build hospitals and nursing homes and built a successful business.

Bill "Woolo" Rusco served in the U. S. Army during WWII and then graduated from Kansas University. He worked at various jobs until his retirement.

Elmer "Peter Rabbit" Rusco earned a bachelor's degree and master's degree in Political Science from Kansas University. After completing his studies, Elmer went to Reno, Nevada and became a professor of political science at the University of Nevada-Reno, where he earned Emeritus status. He was an activist, author, and professor of political science specializing in the civil rights movement. He authored several books on race issues, and the Civil Rights Movement including *Good Time Coming?: Black Nevadans in the Nineteenth Century.*

Jack "Jocko the Magnificent" Clevenger became a business owner when he and his wife bought a diner in Wichita, Kansas. He and his wife operated the diner for many years as a "mom and pop" eatery.

Warren "Dux" Marriage served in the Corps of Army Engineers during WWII and was stationed in Europe. He met and married Joan and returned to Colorado Springs where they raised five children. He was instrumental in designing the large waterlines through the Rocky

Mountains.

Eldon served in the Navy during WWII and graduated from Kansas State University. He returned to the ranch to become a partner with Pop Weaver at the ranch for a few years. After several years of drought, it was not possible to support a wife and four children plus his parents on the ranch. Eldon started a hardware store business in Kiowa, Kansas. Eventually, Eldon was a KSU Extension 4-H Specialist for twenty years in Winfield and Hutchinson serving Kansas youth. During that time he completed a Master's Degree at Colorado State University. He retired to enjoy summers in Kansas, winters in Arizona, and now lives in Colorado.

VACATION TIME
1927

This poem was written by H. Marietta Weaver in September, 1927 for her author's club following the birth of Eldon Ralph Weaver.

They asked us to write a poem
About our vacation time,
Since none spent theirs as I did
Here is my little rhyme.

I attended the last Club meeting
About the middle of May,
I looked so very portly
I wanted to stay away;

But our Club are all so friendly
And not stuck up or proud,
So what causes comment elsewhere
Is encouraged and allowed.

I stayed at home all summer
As I larger and larger grew;
Some thought it would surely be triplets
But others guessed only two.

In spite of my great proportions
Company continued to come,
So I cooked and worked all summer
And wished they had stayed at home.

I kept on growing bigger
Till I waddled when I walked,
And the larger and fatter I became
The more the folks all talked.

Appendix

The floors would shake beneath me,
The chairs would creak and groan,
So I finally went to Greensburg
And left my folks alone.

I arrived at Mrs. Steadman's
Late in the afternoon,
Telegraphic messages up my spine
Said I hadn't come too soon.

'Twas August 18th, about one o'clock
When things began to hum,
Mrs. Steadman called the Doctor
And also the folks at home.

At five that morning a boy arrived,
With a long and lusty shout,
He looked around quite wildly
To see what 'twas all about.

We think he's the finest ever,
Eldon Ralph will be his name,
We hope he'll be a healthy child
And someday achieve great fame.

I greatly enjoyed the next two weeks,
The weather was cool and fine,
My friends were lovely to call on me,
And I had a pleasant time.

And now I'm at home and busy,
And my "five" I am thankful for,
But common sense should tell me
I don't need any more.

Mrs. Marietta Weaver

Like Father, Like Son

Pop often repeated this poem at the Father-Son banquet and it stayed
with me as I raised three sons and a daughter.

"Well, what are you going to be my boy,
When you have reached manhood's years;
A doctor, a lawyer, or actor great,
Moving throngs to laughter and tears?"
But he shook his head as he gave his reply
In a serious way he had:
"I don't think I'd care to be any of them;
I want to be like my Dad!"

He wants to be like his Dad! You men,
Did you ever think as you pause
That the boy who watches your every move
Is building a set of laws?
He's molding a life you're a model for,
And whether it's good or bad
Depends on the kind of example set
To the boy who'd be like his Dad.

Would you have him go everywhere you go?
Have him do just the things you do?
And see everything that your eyes behold,
And woo all the things you woo?
When you see the worship that shines in the eyes
Of your lovable little lad,
Could you rest content if he gets his wish
And grows to be like his Dad?

It's a job that none but yourself can fill;
It's a charge you must answer for;
It's a duty to show him the road to tread
'Ere he reaches his manhood's door.
It's a debt you owe for the greatest joy
On this old earth to be had;
This pleasure of having a boy to raise
Who wants to be like his Dad.

Appendix

G'ma Marriage & Eldon   G'ma Great age 98   Eldon, 6 months

Kenny age 6, Eldon, Dick, and kitty

Kenny, Doris, Vivian, Eldon   Marjorie and Eldon

Grandfather Weaver, Eldon, Gerald, Bernice   Eldon, Bernice, Gerald

Vivian, Doris with Eldon on mule   Eldon, age 5

Eldon. age 10

Grade School Band

5th grade: Eldon, Jack Casper, Glenda Hensley, Gene Rudd, Ralph Copeland

Eldon, age 12

Eldon & Woolo (Bill)

Eldon on Lightning

Eldon, age 11

Eldon, Jerome, Toots & colt 1938

Eldon and pals 1938

Eldon, Wings & colt

Eldon and Doris

Camp-out Pals

Eldon, Pop & King 1939   Eldon & Bill Rusco

Bottle fed calf-Blizzard   Snow drifts at ranch house

Eldon the Gunslinger

Eldon on Trigger

215

Eldon c. 1940   Pop, Mama, Marj, Ken, Doris, Eldon 1939

Eldon c. 1943   Eldon senior photo

Mama, Pop, Eldon 1945   Eldon on Buck c. 1943

Kenny, Eldon 1940   Kenny c. 1940

Kenny Air Corps 1942   Eldon Seaman 1st Class

Marjorie, Doris, Vivian c. 1937

Eagle Canyon Ranch View

Author Biography

Eldon Weaver grew up on Eagle Canyon Ranch, a large cattle ranch operated by his parents, and located south of Mullinville, Kansas. Immediately after graduating from high school in 1945, he enlisted in the U. S. Navy and served during the final months of WWII. He graduated from Kansas State University in 1951 and returned to Mullinville to become a partner with his parents on the ranch. After several years of drought, it was not possible to support a wife and four children plus his parents on the ranch. Eldon started a Gamble's hardware store in Kiowa, Kansas. Eventually, he returned to his agriculture roots as a KSU Extension 4-H Specialist for twenty years in Winfield and Hutchinson. During that time he completed a Master's Degree at Colorado State University. He retired to spend summers in Kansas, winters in Arizona, and now lives in Colorado.

Eldon's writing career began in the 1980s and he has steadily added short stories to his collection of writing. His most recent episodes were written in 2015, at age 87, for the completion of this collection of his favorite memories from his early years.

Stains along edges.
7/19/18 JB

23967042R00127

Made in the USA
San Bernardino, CA
06 September 2015